LOGIC PROBLEM SOLVING

How to solve problems in life

By

Joseph Kane

© 2019 Joseph Kane

All right reserved. No portion of this book may be copied or reproduced in any form without written and signed permission from the publisher, except as permitted by UK copyright law.

Table of Contents

Preface 1
Part 1 – Approach 16
Part 2 – Tools 32
   Tool 1. Reconnaissance 32
   Tool 2. Rabbit hole 35
   Tool 3. Making decisions 38
   Tool 4. Going from moment to moment. 41
   Tool 5. Figuring out and perceiving people 47
   Tool 6. Being resourceful 60
   Tool 7. Visualising ambitions, problems or goals 67
   Tool 8. Keeping composed 74
   Tool 9. Asking the right questions 81
   Tool 10. Answering questions correctly 85
   Tool 11. Everything happens for a reason 90
   Tool 12. Preparation & Pre-emptive action 96
   Tool 13. Logic Expectations 103
   Tool 14. It's all in the detail 110
   Tool 15. Being versatile 120
   Tool 16. Encouraging a change 124
   Tool 17. Making connections 130
Seeing the whole picture 133
Summary 135

Preface

Disclaimer

Before you start reading, the information in this book is for educational purposes only. I, the author, am not a qualified logician, yet I explain about logic to the best of my ability from research. The tool section from this book derives from methods I have created that will help you solve problems using your senses, your environment, and much more. Just because you arrive at a conclusion with a theory, doesn't mean you should act on it. You shouldn't act on, or attempt to solve problems if it breaks the law, causes harm, or damages any property. How you use this knowledge is your responsibility. Although this is a powerful concept to acknowledge, I encourage you to do good with it. Names, characters, and events were created in a fictitious manner to demonstrate examples. The methods and practices involved were put together based on existing facts, knowledge, and data. As a new concept, you will gain a better mindset using critical thinking. You, the reader, do not have to accept or apply this method if you choose not to. By continuing to read this book, you agree to act accordingly to this disclaimer.

Why choose this book?

This book was written to benefit everyone. If you want to make better decisions, understand life easier, achieve your goals, and overcome problems, then this book will do just that. With this new mindset, you will have the power to:

1. Become rich
2. Have better relationships
3. Understand how things work
4. Live a peaceful life
5. Become popular
6. Overcome challenges
7. Solve almost any problem
8. Make better decisions
9. Start your dream business
10. Be the person you want to be

These seem like big promises, and they are, but wait and see what kind of resolve you have by the time you finish this book. Anyone reading this is expected to lead with an open mind, possess a willingness to accept truths and realities, and be able to adapt to sudden changes. It's also for those who want to progress, learn, and to work through problems logically. If you are a narrow-minded person that can't accept facts, realities, and truths, then I'm afraid you will struggle to apply this concept to your life. If you do not want to work through a process that could reveal further problems, then this might not be suitable for you. Logic problem-solving consists of going down the rabbit hole to create a big picture, reveal the exact causes of the problem, then taking the steps needed to work through them before concluding. It's not easy facing challenges, but necessary to understand what we are dealing with if we want to overcome them.

Only attempt what you feel comfortable with when facing sensitive or private events in your life. The best benefit about this skill and mindset is that you will have a better understanding of what's going on around you, even if you don't wish to act on it. Start with minor issues in your life, then work your way up to more significant problems. The best part is, no one is right or wrong. There is no single route to a conclusion, and the possibilities are endless. When you figure out how to apply this to your life, you will make better decisions, be happier, and stand out from the crowd. I will show you how to be diverse, dynamic, and flexible from moment to moment that will lead you to success in everything you do. You will not find a book out there that shows you how to think for yourself with such a perspective. I have written this in simple terms for everyone to understand, using straightforward examples that we already do in life using our senses, our brain, and our will power.

What is logic problem-solving?

Logic problem solving is a method I have put together that identifies the problem, cause, or focus, then finds where it is coming from before finding a solution using a wide range of tools. After reading the tool section, you will be as thorough as a detective, as precise as a marksman, and as resourceful as a survivalist. This book is not about basic problem-solving; it's a lifestyle and a mindset if you decide to apply it to your life. It will change the way you think forever. I explain each tool with stories and examples that relate to what you see and do every day. I will show you how to explore every possibility, and how to use your surroundings to your advantage. By using logic to find valid arguments, as well as using our imagination, we can build a picture that reveals the weak link in the chain. Working our way backwards, we find connections related to the problem, and then we use several tools to overcome it.

These tools will be your superpowers, and with great power, comes great responsibility. No Joke! This information is very powerful stuff that shouldn't be abused. Don't interfere or play with someone's life unless its for good purposes. A good problem solver learns to anticipate issues before they happen, but that comes with patience if you stick with it. It is estimated that the average person makes 35,000 decisions every day. Big or small, we are constantly faced with new challenges. Don't ever panic or worry the next time a problem presents itself. Where there's a will, there's a way. All you have to do is use logic once I have re-wired your brain. The better the imagination you have, the more possibilities you will create for yourself before you approach a challenge. The more problems you solve in different aspects of your life, the more familiar you will become the next time they happen. Thinking is fun when using this concept. The only downside to critical thinking is that it zaps your brainpower, making you feel tired, so don't overuse it. Get ready to look behind the scenes to see the driving force behind all the questions you have in life. There is often a reason behind something that happens, and you will be able to identify that if you wish to continue.

Does this sound familiar? "What do I do? How do I do it? Where do I go? I'm confused. I need help. I'm not good at anything. I'm useless. I want it, but I can't do it because I've tried. It's impossible. It can't be achieved." All of these statements are forever present until you learn how to free your mind. The greatest gift you can ever receive is the ability to think for yourself.

Once you have finished working your way through, you will never think the same again. It's easy and straightforward once you get the gist of it. Learning this concept and changing your mindset feels terrific, but wait until you use it. It will turn an average thinker into half a genius. Most of the time, I go through life relaxed without utilising my own skills, but whenever a problem arises, I flick my logic problem-solving skills on like a light switch. The results I get are remarkable. I'm at a stage in life where I'm focussed, happy, organised, and content along with many other positives. We drift through life without knowing what to do, where to go, or why we should do it; it's like the blind leading the blind. How would you feel if I told you this book will make you rich, famous, stress-free, powerful, happy, and the best thing since sliced bread? The question is, how far are you willing to go? What are you willing to sacrifice? Do you wish to achieve great things, or do you just want a smooth ride to old age? The possibilities are endless. Of course, I can't do it for you, but once you know how to think for yourself, and learn how to approach problems logically, nothing will stand in your way.

There is, however, a small percentage of problems that can't be achieved. Missed opportunities, unpredictable events, or a change of circumstances can ruin our plans. Don't let that put you off for one second. Like anything else in life, there is never any certainty. As long as you are ready to face change, realities, and facts, you will do just fine. Become an independent thinker with a direction. Everyone around you will be blown away with how wise you seem to be, and how you seem to know so much information. Top-flight professional sports men and women perform great results, week in, week out because they have crafted their skills over the years. Businesses become successful because they have identified the value they offer, they know the professionalism they provide, and they know when to scale up using their initiative. It is the same for logic problem solvers; we know when to act, how to act, and why we should act.

Hopefully, this book will inspire you to do great things, encourage you to face any problem, and help become the person you want to be, instead of doing what everyone expects you to do. If you can imagine it, you can create it. I have plans for my life that seem light-years away, when in fact, they are in touching distance. You can do the same too. I don't just solve problems, I dissect them, toy with them, and manipulate them in my favour. Don't worry though, if you wish to continue I have made all my examples relatable. All you have to do is study the tools I present to you. Once you know what you are doing, you can look at every single aspect of your life in frames per second, just like an old movie reel. Please note, because we are unearthing the cause of a problem, further problems will appear. These generally need to be solved first; it's like getting rid of weeds in a garden, we need to kill the roots, or they will keep growing back. That's why people tend to stick their head in the sand, its because they know that other issues need to be solved first. If you're not ready to face those challenges, then come back to that specific problem another time when you feel up to it.

Why I wrote this book

I first decided to write this book a few years before I actually got round to doing it. I left it for so long because I didn't know where to start. It's incredible how thoughts, experience, and knowledge turn into an idea, that becomes a concept, then ends up being a book. The tools I've developed are a representation of my newly found strengths. I eventually started writing when my life drastically improved. There were so many unanswered questions; now there's nothing I don't understand. When I started typing away on my computer, I was able to turn ideas into actionable methods that relate to people. I almost didn't write this book for concerns the information within would be abused, but the benefits outweighed the negatives. It can help someone overcome or achieve anything they wish. All you have to do is look closely, be patient, and meet certain conditions with an open mind.

As a young boy, my family thought it was better to keep the truth from me. They thought they were protecting me by lying, when in reality, it did more damage than good. Because my life was kept in the dark, I suffered tremendously. Learning the hard way, I was kicked out of two high schools for messing around in class. Algebra, science and every other lesson I attended didn't benefit my life for one second. Years later, it dawned on me that maths and english were essential for everyday task, but everything else in my view was nothing more than general knowledge. Nothing prepared me for the real world. What they don't teach you in school are things like life skills, how to survive on the streets, or how to think for yourself. They failed to tell me how life suddenly becomes a battle every morning once your feet hit the ground. I had no idea what to do with myself and was left feeling an alien on my own planet. Trying to work things out for myself was impossible because I didn't know where to start. My only option was to copy and follow everyone around me who had no hope or direction themselves. I soon realised that money makes the world go round, people climb on each other to get higher in society, and it's every man for himself. To learn that the Battle of Hastings happened a thousand years ago in 1066, had no bearing on my life whatsoever. Fast forward to my 30th birthday a few years ago; I still didn't know how to think for myself. Then, one day, something amazing happened…

…The radio came on.

Driving down the road with my Uncle, still confused and unable to think for myself, I heard on the radio that the human brain thinks logically. My curiosity was aroused. I wanted to be able to figure things out for myself without someone having to tell me what, how and why. My Uncle thinks he is smart, and that everyone else is thick because he knows a lot of general knowledge, yet send him to the shop for bread and milk, and he comes back with cheese and eggs. As time went on, I couldn't get the word "logic" out of my head. I began pondering for days, weeks, even months creating brain waves like solar flares from the sun. At the time, the main focus of my life was all the problems I had. After much thought, I started to work through them one by one. Instead of being content, I thought bigger and deeper.

Logic might be familiar to most people, but to me, it was the missing key. Before long, I developed a blueprint of conditions to be met in order to achieve the results I wanted. Once my troubles were solved, I took it to the next level. Then I started to have better relationships, made accomplishments that seemed impossible, and became the person I always wanted to be. My life improved in leaps and bounds, but that isn't to say it was easy. I sacrificed by making massive changes. Although logic is nothing new, the tools I've created coexist nicely by producing some impressive results.

Over the next three years of profound thinking, I was able to shape my life like water in a glass. Now, I can predict to some extent, manufacture a problem, and even pre-emptively make decisions to avert the problem in the first place. There is never any certainty to accomplishing what you want, however, if the logical conditions are met, and the tools I have provided are utilised, then the possibility to achieve an objective is pretty much guaranteed. Keep in mind it's not for the faint-hearted. In theory, there is always a way to overcome problems, goals, and ambitions, but that doesn't mean you should act on every finding.

How to study this book

The first thing you need to learn and understand is logic, I'm going to keep it short, sweet, and straightforward. You need to be able to validate arguments before moving on to the next section. After a brief introduction to logic, I will show you the tools of the trade to asses situations, plan a course of action, and how to execute a plan. Each tool stands on its own with examples, yet you can use as many tools as you want to solve problems. By the time you reach the end of this book, if you don't feel ready or confident, you might want to consider going over it again. I suggest you read this book at least twice. Once you have the right mindset and practised what you know, you will officially become a logic problem solver. The bulletins below are a short description of the tools we will cover. Don't worry if they don't make sense, all will be revealed. Keep this book handy for future reference, just as I do:

- How to investigate a problem to make it easier to solve.
- Making the right decisions that lead you down the correct path.
- Acting accordingly during each moment to get a calculated outcome.

- Assess a person or a situation to work out what's coming next.
- Asking the right questions to find the correct answers.
- Answering the right questions to avoid making the situation worse.
- Countering a problem correctly based on what's already happened.
- Visualising ambitions, problems or goals for an advantage to assist you.
- Keeping composed under pressure in certain situations.
- Finding connections between everything that happens.
- Preparing before a problem and how to pre-emptively take action.
- Using logic expectations from your surroundings to use to your advantage.
- Being versatile and adaptable to make changes when necessary.

What you will take from this book

Once you have finished studying this concept, your brain will re-wire itself to be able to think logically first and foremost. Even before you get to the tools section, your mind will race like a horse. I spent three years mastering this idea, concept, and mindset, and now I want to give it to the world. This book will help you get to where you want to be in life. The possibilities of what you can achieve or endless. Being enlightened as I once was, you will be able to identify the necessary steps to succeed. Once you grasp it, then apply it to your daily life, you will see the benefits from your new approach that's far superior to your peers. By adopting this mindset as a lifestyle, you will find everything starts to fall into place. Being so accustomed to using your heart and emotions, you will learn how to use your head instead. Here are some benefits from being a logic problem solver:

- Read a situation before it happens
- Think logically 24/7 as a default
- Read body language before someone acts
- Assess situations methodically
- Make better conditions around a problem
- Predict an event to some extent before it happens
- Resolve issues before and after they happen
- Reach your goals, ambitions, and dreams with light work
- Use your head instead of emotions
- Succeed in love, money, and relationships
- Become resourceful
- Use situations to your advantage

- Achieve things that seem impossible or beyond your reach
- Become the person you always wanted to be
- Fulfil dreams you never thought were realistic
- Have skills that your peers or opposition won't have

With many more benefits, this is the tip of the iceberg. It will change the decisions you make forever. It's pretty cool knowing that I'm about to change the course of your life, but that's precisely what will happen. Get ready to be an efficient problem solver, precise, organised, equipped, resourceful, successful, powerful, and smarter than you have ever been. You can thank me later, but for now, get your thinking cap on and let's get started.

Part 1 – Approach

When you went to school, what did they teach you? Before you answer, teaching is precisely the problem I'm talking about. Instead of being taught how to think for yourself, you were educated in certain subjects that correlate with employment once you leave school. Most of us were educated by state-funded schools that follow the National Curriculum. The government wants you to be educated so that you can get a job. Once you get a job, you can pay tax that goes towards royalty, politicians, and makes countries wealthy enough to have worldwide influence. It's not a coincidence or an opinion; it's a valid argument based on true facts. Without workers, there would be no businesses. Without a government, there would be no one to pay tax to. In my view, the government will not pay for an education that teaches you how to think for yourself. The mind is the most powerful tool a human can possess. The last thing a government wants is its citizens asking too many questions, or rebelling against its ideology. Some countries control their citizens with fear or repression. Alcohol killed 7,697 people in 2017 in the UK. There used to be a pub on every corner. Keeping workers happy and fuelled seems too convenient for me. The closest you will come to an education that teaches you how to think for yourself is university. There, you will learn how to do research, develop arguments, and study critical thinking. School is compulsory, and university is optional but only if you can afford it. It would be great if we were taught how to think for ourselves at a young age, but sadly it's not the case. Even parents can only teach what they know. So, let's get stuck in. Here are some examples of the problems we face in life:

1. Getting a job.
2. Finding a partner.
3. Meeting new friends.
4. Finding a home.
5. Becoming better at sport.
6. Starting a business.
7. Dealing with people.
8. Trying to get out of debt.
9. Overcoming bad habits.
10. Taking too many risks

These problems might be big and broad, but believe it or not, they are easy to overcome. The more challenging issues occur when situations derive from more than one problem at the same time, like complicated relationships or problems thrown at our feet with no time to think. Challenging times begin when you need to do something that makes you feel uncomfortable. You will find yourself conflicted between sacrifice, boundaries, and what you believe to be right and wrong. When using logic, anythings possible as long as you can push your morals, principles, and ethics to one side. That doesn't mean you should carry out every plan you create; it just means you have come to a conclusion. Having an understanding, or knowing you have a plan can be enough to reassure you. It can be comforting knowing that you have the power to solve issues without acting on them.

Using logic to make valid arguments, we can establish facts and truths to make decisions. Like a detective building a picture of a murder scene, we need to analyse every action, every thought, and every possibility. The logic section is important because it helps us understand what's going on, why it's happening, and what we need to do. There is a reason behind what happens in life, and coincidences rarely occur, so let's not take them into account. You can also make poor decisions in life that are emotionally motivated, or because of a set of beliefs you have. The tools we will go over are self-explanatory, so let's get the boring stuff out of the way.

What is logic?

Logic is a science that studies the principles of correct and incorrect reasoning. It's not a matter of opinion but evaluates reasoning and arguments to find a conclusion. Logicians want to understand what makes a good argument, and what makes a bad one. It helps us to avoid mistakes in our own reasoning as well as others, making us better thinkers. Humans have been thinking logically since early existence. The only problem was, humans couldn't distinguish the logical from the illogical. Nowadays, we have general principles and rules to follow for the best reasoning thanks to Aristotle, a Greek philosopher who was the first logician. By taking data or information, we can determine whether theories are right or wrong. Using logic, we can evaluate what conclusion is legitimate or illegitimate from what we already know. This is essential for making decisions, working out problems, and reaching goals as you will soon discover.

Different kinds of logic

There are several types of logic; the most familiar ones are "deductive" and "inductive." An argument has one or more premises but only one conclusion. Both the premise and the conclusion are truth-bearers, each capable of being true or false, but not both. Feel free to experiment with different kinds of logic.

Deductive reasoning

Deductive reasoning is a process of reasoning from one or more statements, also known as premises, to reach a logically certain conclusion. Deductive reasoning goes in the same direction as the conditions met, and links premises with conclusions. If all premises are true, then the conclusion reached is necessarily true. Deductive reasoning is sometimes referred to as top-down logic.

Examples of Deductive Reasoning:

- All dolphins are mammals. All mammals have kidneys. Therefore, all dolphins have kidneys.
- All dogs have a good sense of smell. Bailey is a dog. Therefore, Bailey has a good sense of smell.
- It's dangerous to drive on icy streets. The streets are icy now, so it would be dangerous to drive.

Inductive reasoning

Inductive reasoning is an approach to logical thinking that involves making generalisations based on specific details from experience, observation or facts. While the conclusion of a deductive argument is certain, the truth from the conclusion of an inductive argument is only probable based on evidence given. Inductive reasoning is sometimes referred to as bottom-up logic.

Examples of inductive logic:

- My mother is Irish. She has blonde hair. Therefore, everyone from Ireland has blonde hair.
- Most of our snowstorms come from the north. It's starting to snow. This snowstorm must be coming from the north.
- Max is a shelter dog. He is happy. All shelter dogs are happy.

So, why is all this important? Because it helps you find the correct answers by asking the right questions, to then arrive at the right conclusion every time you take on a problem. If your wife or husband needed help with a bad habit, you can't lie to them because you don't want to hurt their feelings, you need to use logical reasoning to do what's required before the habit destroys them. Think of logic as a mediator to help you come to a conclusion without having to get personally involved, or by taking sides. It can also stop you from presuming, guessing, or thinking you are correct all the time.

Each decision you make has consequences, so if you don't make the best decisions possible, how can you expect to resolve or overcome anything in your life?

What is a logical argument?

A logical argument is a process of creating a statement from one or more existing statements known as premises, that proceeds to a conclusion. While statements may be considered as either true or false, an argument may be regarded as either valid or invalid. Using certain guiding principles or procedures, we hope to arrive at the desired conclusion. We present ideas that are consistent and coherent. An argument derives of:

- Proposition
- Premise
- Conclusion

1. A proposition is the beginning of your argument or the statement you are trying to prove. For example, suppose you want to argue the point that you are scared to approach women. This is your opening statement or proposition from which you will build on. It is equivalent to a hypothesis. We start with a proposition when we

want to create arguments, but it's also useful for solving problems as you will soon see.

2. The premise is the statement or statements that follow the proposition. Your premise is basically your evidence or reasons used to justify the proposition. In our example, you would look at some of the reasons as to why you are scared to approach women. One of the reasons might be because you had a bad experience the last time you tried. Now that you have a hypothesis, you can move on to the conclusion.

3. After you have started your proposition, and presented evidence known as the premise, you will arrive at a conclusion. In this case, you are scared of approaching women because you've had bad experiences, putting you off from trying again in the future. In logic problem solving, we use conclusions to make the best decisions possible. We might not always be right, but it's essential to be as accurate as possible.

Please note that the proposition, premise, and conclusion are only used for validating logical arguments in chronological order, however, when we initially attempt to solve a problem, we use a different type of logic called "Backward Induction."

Starting with the conclusion, we work our way back until we discover the root cause as I'm about to explain below.

Backward induction

Backward induction is a process of reasoning backwards starting with potential conclusions. The conclusion, in our case, is the problem, focus, or goal that we want to achieve. This is my foundation for solving problems, so remember this well; it will be the starting point every single time. Once we have our eyes on the problem itself, we can work backwards in reverse-chronological order to find the premise, then the proposition. When a detective arrives at a murder scene, they investigate to build a picture, before working backwards until they know how, when, and why it happened. It's important for numerous reasons: we can find any connections, see the driving force behind it, notice any weaknesses to exploit, and much more. Things generally don't just happen. We must surmise that there is a logical explanation. Working our way backwards can reveal new problems, so be prepared to deal with them if you wish to overcome the main issue. Try to think of it as unravelling a ball of string full of knots. People give up when they realise many issues need to be solved before solving the main problem, but that's life; no one said it's easy.

"In logic, there are no morals." - Rudolf Carnap

Well done!

The hard part is over, believe it or not. Instead of thinking you know best, or tormenting yourself with what you believe to be true, you can now make valid arguments. This logic problem-solving concept that I proudly created operates like NASA, and just like NASA, everything has to be down to perfection and checked three times. We don't have to be as strict, but the attitude remains the same. Let no question go unanswered, and let no rock be unturned. Every problem takes us on a reverse-chronological journey until we find the cause, weakness, or characteristic to use to our advantage. People are driven by a need or an emotion using very little brainpower. There has to be a purpose for a series of events going on. When I show you the tools to weigh everything up, you might even outsmart me! Once you learn this skill, it will awaken your brain like never before. You will never look at people or situations the same way ever again.

After some practice, using this method becomes second nature. There is nothing better than finding the driving force behind a problem, or knowing what motivates a person to act the way they do. There is no better satisfaction overcoming challenges all by yourself without any help. It's fantastic having an open mind to see every aspect before accomplishing a goal. Get ready to become rich and do nothing all day once you find out who is making all the money, where you can find people to do the work for you, and how to scale up. Get ready to have great relationships with people because you know what's coming. Expect an awesome life for taking the initiative to act, instead of not doing enough to help yourself. Kiss goodbye to your old narrowminded personality that got you nowhere for following rules, or based on what you think to be correct. Stand out from the crowd by being your own mastermind.

How can we use logic to solve problems? Well, logic is great for guiding us like a beacon. Its good for validating arguments, but helps us reveal the causes. We aim to understand as much as possible, and to learn as much as possible before making a single decision. When logic takes you down different paths, look carefully, or you will miss valuable clues no matter how small or irrelevant they seem to be. One way to think about it is if you go to the toilet during a movie. When you return, you won't fully understand the rest of the film because you've missed a few scenes. Here are a few questions to ask yourself:

1. What's the problem?

2. What do I want to achieve?
3. What are the obstacles stopping me from reaching my goal?
4. What information do I already know?
5. What information don't I know?
6. What am I capable of?
7. What can't I do?
8. What am I willing to give?
9. How much am I willing to sacrifice?
10. Is there a weakness?

Some of these questions will already come into your thoughts every time there is a challenge. You might be able to work things out for yourself, but when doing so, there is a good chance you're not utilising all of your brainpower. You may have failed to cover every aspect, or you're unable to take everything into account. Most of us barely scratch the surface of our troubles because we are restricted by many factors. We tend to be our own worst enemy. Here are three examples to get you warmed up:

1. Stan works for a company that he loves but receives a low salary. After receiving a new job offer with better pay, it's not something he would enjoy, and will stop him from spending time with his family due to the four-hour-long

journey. Unfortunately, he is torn between using his head and his heart. Stan wants to make more money for his family's future but decides that happiness is more important, so he stays in the job he's in. Being a logic problem solver, he wonders if it's possible to make more money with the job he loves. Already a manager, he realises that the best way to make more money is to buy some shares. That way, he can own some of the company, receive dividends each year, and hopefully get a promotion. Stan's initial problem to make more money has now turned into three problems. Firstly, he needs to get a loan or a part-time job to be able to buy some shares. Secondly, he needs to complete some courses that will further qualify him. Over time, Stan becomes more qualified to take on more responsibilities and finds enough money to buy some shares. By solving two of the three problems, Stan's goal to make more money with the company he loves is becoming a reality. Years later, Stan bought enough shares to own the company outright. Applying his skills, he built a chain of stores worldwide, making him super-rich and able to spend as much time with his family as he wanted.

2. Rachel receives a low income but needs some new clothes. When she goes shopping, everything is

expensive, leaving her with not much money for food. That's a problem because she can't afford it. Instead of paying retail prices, she uses logic problem solving to find out why it's expensive, and how she can save money. After researching online, she discovers that the clothes she buys are made in a factory in China, costing a fraction of the price. Now she knows the real value she decides to buy directly from China saving a fortune on clothes. Because Rachel has learnt a little about business, such as buy low, sell high, and how two companies are making a profit out of her, she uses that to her advantage. Her problem was solved, and now she buys most things from China, saving plenty of money. By doing this, she is going directly to the source instead of being the last link in the chain.

3. Mick has bought broadband internet for his home, but the speed he gets is very slow. He justifies the problem believing that's how it's meant to be. Once he applies logic problem solving, he decides to ring up the provider to investigate. A customer service agent explains that he's getting the right speed for what he's paying for, and refused to cancel his contract. After looking deeper into the service he receives, he finds that the speeds are not what he is paying for, and the customer service

representative lied to him about being stuck in a contract. Armed with the correct information from the terms and conditions, along with his consumer rights, he phoned back to talk to the manager. Because Mick recorded the conversation when he was lied to and now knows what his consumer rights are, the manager gave Mick twelve months of free internet with speeds of 100mbs, which is SUPER FAST!

Now we have covered logic, approaches to new challenges, and looked at some examples to help you think along the right lines, let's move on to the main section of this book. In part two, I will show you all the tools that you need for facing problems, challenges, and goals. Each tool is self-explanatory that creates a powerful mindset to equip you with what you need. I've provided relatable examples from everyday life to learn easier. By the time you reach the last tool, you will be able to use all of your senses, be able to assess situations, use your environment to your advantage, and much more. You need to presume that there is a logical explanation for everything that happens. It's perfectly fine concluding, no matter how unpractical or unethical it might seem. Conclusions can remain theories without having to act on them. Please remember that this is for educational purposes only. Broaden your mind, take everything into account, be patient, and try to think beyond your imagination. Armed with a variety of skills and abilities, nothing will stop you from succeeding. Have fun, get creative, and see what kind of results you get. Good luck!

"Things don't just happen; people make them happen."
– Zig Ziglar

Part 2 – Tools

Tool 1. Reconnaissance

Before trying to solve anything, the best thing you can do is gather as much information as possible. Before carrying out an operation, armed forces carry out a process of obtaining information about the enemy. By sending out a small task force, soldiers discretely find out what they are up against, where the weaknesses are, if they can be exploited, and what they need in order to counter the threat. Once the survey is over, the probability of success is much higher. It might seem silly, pointless, or overkill for some circumstances, but take my word for it, even the smallest bit of information can reveal a complex network of connections to the problem in question, especially if it comes back to haunt you. Reflect on some of these considerations during your probe:

- When, where, and why did it occur?
- Look into circumstances around it.
- Find out who or what is involved.
- Look for weaknesses to use to your advantage.
- Use technology as your friend.
- Ask questions or research on Google to reveal more.

- Study methodically to avoid missing any key points.
- Take notes on smaller problems that could get in the way.
- What does the problem do? What are the characteristics?
- Find any connections that are related, no matter how big or small.
- Look at what you are capable of, and what you will need to overcome it.
- Reflect on preparations for what you need to do.

By surveying, we can assess if we are capable of solving the problem, find out what's needed, how long it might take, and other essential factors to take into consideration. Watch and listen with due care and attention. We can discover what we are willing to give, and we can find out what lengths we are willing to go to. Your mission is to gather as must intel as possible to be able to make the best decisions when needed. Once you have gathered enough data, this is what you should know:

- Knowledge about the topic or subject you are facing, to be able to counter it.
- A plan ready to carry out knowing what the consequences will be.
- Preparation for losing what you are willing to sacrifice.

- How external factors play a part, and if there could be any unexpected inconveniences during the process.
- Are there any discrepancies you could use in your favour?
- Will any actions make the situation worse, or cause further issues?
- Will there be any collateral damage or harm to anyone else involved?
- When and how you will approach the problem.

Knowledge and understanding means we will have more options for overcoming the problem with a high success rate. It gives us leverage that we never had before. Don't rush in if you think you can solve it straight away. A logic problem solver should be efficient, patient, and tries to keep implications to a minimum. Use some or all of these tools to create an action plan before executing it. Don't set a timescale; it will take as long as it needs to. It doesn't matter if the parcel company misplaced your package, or you're in the middle of a divorce; a problem is a problem, you never know how big it could become, or if the problem will return.

"Time spent in reconnaissance is seldom wasted."
– John Marsden

Tool 2. Rabbit hole

Going down the Rabbit hole refers to logically figuring out a problem. Starting with the focus, problem, or goal, we first investigate with what we have, and then we work our way back until we reveal the connections to create a picture. Things don't just happen; there must be a logical reason behind why it exists, excluding any coincidences. Remember what we covered about proposition, premise, and conclusion? Well, that's great for validating arguments in chronological order, but this is when we use backward induction to start with a potential conclusion for reasoning backwards. In this example, Tim is met with problems that can only be overcome by investigating. Also, notice how solving one issue turns into several more, sending him on a wild goose chase until he gets to the bottom of it:

- Tim checks his bank account to find that £500 has been taken without his knowledge. He now has the task of finding out what happened to his money. As a logic problem solver, he investigates to get to the root cause. The first step is to call his bank. The bank manager explains that the money was taken out by a car rental company. Not knowing where his card was, and confident he didn't spend the money himself, he needs to go deeper down the rabbit hole to find out more information. With the bank blocking his card on suspicion of fraud, Tim calls his wife. With no answer, he now has two problems. Until he speaks to his wife, he can't find out if she has spent the money. Driving home to look for her, Tim ran out of petrol. He realised that he doesn't have any money until his new card arrives in the post, and he can't go back to the bank because it's closed. Now there are four problems, and the rabbit hole is getting deeper by the minute. When he reaches his house on foot, he finds his new wife on the driveway in a new car. It turned out that his wife's car had broken down, so she hired one. Because she picked up Tim's card by accident instead of hers, she had no choice but to use it. Luckily, Tim's sister works at the car rental business, so his wife didn't need much documentation. His wife lent him some money until his new card arrived solving all of his problems.

On this occasion, the problem solved itself. As you can see, each focus, problem, or goal has its own set of propositions, premises, and conclusions. Solving one problem can lead to new ones, forcing us to start the process over and over, before getting to the root cause. Now you know some of the foundations for logic problem solving, let's look at other tools. In nearly every case, we will start with backward induction because it gives us something to work with. Sometimes, we don't have much to go on, so we use our imagination along with other tools, but don't worry, no challenge is too big.

"If you go too far down the rabbit-hole of what people think about you, it can change everything about who you are." - Taylor Swift

Tool 3. Making decisions

Every decision you contemplate or decide to act on will lead you down a particular path. You can use logic, go with your conscience, go with your heart, or make decisions based on emotions. If possible, have a plan that leads to the result you want. That way, you will have some certainty on what's to come. Sometimes, situations can go moment to moment, causing you to rethink the whole process again. If that's the case, try to be careful, adaptable, and patient. For every decision, there will be consequences that create new possibilities. Making decisions can be tough, especially if you are presented with more than one choice. Take everything into consideration. If there is more than one choice, you might want to use your head instead of your heart, and never act on something that leads to negative consequences. You will solve problems better if you don't bring emotions into the mix, or get personally involved. Take a look at this predicament that Jane is in:

- Jane lives with her mum while she saves up to buy her first house. Her boyfriend lives in a bedsit and receives a low income but wants Jane to move in with him. If she decides to move in, she risks spending her savings, leaving her unable to put a deposit down on a house.

What should she do? Should she use her heart and move in with her boyfriend, who's situation could cause her to spend her savings, or should she pursue stability by getting her first house? We are all free to choose our destiny. Bricks might last longer, giving her security, yet love can be a beautiful thing. Jane decided to move in with her boyfriend. Twelve months later, the deposit she had saved up was gone, and her boyfriend left her for another woman. She wanted to move back into her mother's house, but her mum moved to Spain. Now Jane is homeless with nowhere to go. The new problem of being homeless led to countless more issues like depression, anxiety, and losing her job. Not wanting to upset her mum with shame, she kept it to herself.

As you can see, decisions cause consequences that create problems. After making a bad decision, Jane is not a bad person, or in the wrong for going with her heart, she just chose the path that she wanted. If her boyfriend was already financially secure, and they were married, Jane would have more certainty for her security. By saving for a deposit at her mums, she had more control but decided not to use logic problem-solving. Decision making is never easy.

Throughout our life, we will be torn between decisions based on love, feelings, and emotions. Some people can be driven by greed, desperation, addiction, and other undesirable factors. All I can say is be careful. If possible, try to think things through logically. That is easier said than done, but if you can, you should; we are only human after all. As I said before, you don't have to act on something that makes you feel uncomfortable. Solving a problem theoretically can remain a hypothesis leaving you reassured. It comes down to what you are willing to sacrifice, and what lengths you will go to to solve the problem, presuming that is your objective.

"Stay committed to your decisions, but stay flexible in your approach." – Tony Robbins

Tool 4. Going from moment to moment.

To understand this tool, let me introduce you to a quote by Bruce Lee. If you don't know who Bruce Lee is, he was a martial artist, a philosopher, and an actor. He once said in a movie, "If my opponent expands, I contract. When he contracts, I expand." This quote got me thinking. To me, this statement is about re-evaluating every situation after a new development or adapting to changes in new circumstances. Once applying this to logic problem solving, I got some pretty amazing results. The best way to capture a moment is by slowing everything down in slow motion. This started as an idea to evaluate each moment during situations until I did some research, where I then discovered "motion analysis." Funny enough, my findings came up with methods relating to motion and photography. High-speed cameras capture moving images with exposures of less than one second. Then I realised how it's carried out during a test. You have probably seen it on TV when a car drives fast towards a wall with a test dummy inside, then crashes while a camera records it in slow motion. It's also used for things like ballistic firearm studies on 3D models. Investigators used a 3D model to work out how JFK was assassinated, measuring the distance and direction. Here are two examples of assessing situations as you go from moment to moment. They explain how to mentally slow everything down so that it's much easier to evaluate individual actions, developments, or progressions within the situation you are in:

- My favourite sport is boxing. Good fights are few and far between, but when they happen, I gather round the TV on a Saturday night to watch two guys punch the living daylights out of each other. Being a logic problem solver, I am continually thinking, trying to find ways for one of the boxers to win. Problems and goals are slightly different from one another. With a problem, you have to solve it. With a goal, you are driven and determined to succeed to the best of your ability. When I watch fights, I slow everything down in my head like a slow-motion camera. Just as predators watch their prey, I look for a weakness that isn't being protected. I start noticing mistakes that should be exploited, and then I get mad when a boxer sticks to a game plan because their coach told them to. My mind becomes a 3D printer moving around in a fourth dimension. It's frustrating seeing one of the boxers become weaker because they won't adapt. Professional fighters tend to use the correct distance, know when to evade, and know when to counter. You could be the worst boxer in the world, yet still work out how long it will take to bring your arms up to protect your head, from the time it takes an opponent to land a punch, based on distance. Slowing movement down can reveal a ton of information. Every split second of every movement should be accounted for. It's also important to know what you need to do to win. Hitting someone behind the ear can be enough to stun them before going for the knockout. Throwing a punch can leave a part of the body vulnerable for just a second. If you were to wind one of the boxers with a kidney shot, preventing them from fighting back, then unleashed a flurry of punches, the referee would likely stop the fight. Even if an opponent took his eyes off you for just a moment, you would throw a punch. When and how to act has to come down to absolute perfection as much as possible.

A logic problem solver considers themselves and an opponent as one entity, moving around together like improvised choreography, looking for opportunities and weaknesses. Every single second creates a new equation, bringing with it a ray of possibilities. Leaving nothing to chance, in this situation, we would take gravity, distance, time, weight, force, and movement into account. We would also use factors of what will happen, what could happen, what's expected, and how the referee responds, etc. Mixing all of this knowledge as we go from moment to moment, will help you make new decisions every second. You could even include emotions, weather, and physics. This tool can be applied to goals, ambitions, and problems.

Don't create problems by trying to fight fire with fire. By using this tool, you can predict to some extent, make informed decisions, overcome situations, and gain all the advantage you need; let's be honest, I doubt many people will be as methodical as a logic problem solver. A punch is not just a punch; it first starts with a decision in the brain. This tool can be applied to lots of scenarios in your life, so study, analyse, improvise, and adapt if you wish to overcome.

What we just covered focusses more on physical action. A verbal example would be something like an argument or disagreement. I want to show you how to make decisions based on an expectation during a verbal exchange. Take a look at Paul and Ian's story:

- Paul and Ian are good friends that live together, but sometimes they argue. Sharing a flat creates tension between them. Ian is quite messy at times, leaving things wherever they land on the floor. Paul, on the other hand, is a clean freak and finds himself cleaning up after Ian. Because Ian has learnt about logic problem solving, instead of defusing a situation based on tell-tale signs, indications, evidence, or knowledge, he manufactures a scenario to get a reaction out of Paul. He knows Paul has a bad back, hates a messy home, and gets angry when people don't listen to him. While Paul is out, Ian puts rubbish and dirty laundry all over the living room floor. He places some of it under the sofa while remaining visible. When Paul returns home, he finds the mess and confronts Ian, who's sat on the sofa playing on his phone, pretending to ignore him.

Paul: What the heck, Ian, what is this mess?

Ian: ......

Paul: Answer me? How did it get so messy, I only cleaned up last night?

Ian: ......

Paul: Will you answer me! Oh my god, why is it all under the sofa? How am I supposed to clean that with a bad back? You are taking the piss!

Ian: .....

Paul: Why are you just sitting there on your phone, will you answer me and clean this mess up!?

Ian: haha

Ian's theory worked as he thought. Paul went mad because Ian ignored him, was not happy about the mess, and complained about his bad back. He weighed up the situation to figure out what was likely to happen. If someone acts irrational or abusive, there must be a reason for it. Receiving a heads up before something bad happens, even if it's a gut feeling, can save you from a lot of trouble.

"Life was always a matter of waiting for the right moment to act." – Paulo Coelho

Tool 5. Figuring out and perceiving people

The ability to read others will notably affect how you deal with them. When you understand how another person is feeling, you can purvey your message through communication to make sure it is received in the best way possible. Based on how we portray and pass judgement on others from the way they act, what we already know about them, and what we know to be accurate can determine what to expect. We are not psychic of course, but from our perception, we assume there is a logical reason for what someone says or does. Someone could be hiding behind a facade, an image, or has an agenda giving off false signals; even if they are, it won't stop us from figuring that person out. Don't concentrate on what their motive is; we may reveal their intentions eventually; however, it's not essential for figuring someone out at this stage. It is important to understand why people say and do the things they do so that we can counteract with them. If you are not good at dealing with people like me and don't know how to act in front of them, you could be exposing yourself to avoidable problems. Don't worry too much though, this tool will help you.

We can start the process of working someone out from a single word spoken, or by a single action; you just need to look and listen acutely. No matter how boring or irrelevant a conversation seems, revealing information can be gathered. If you reflect afterwards on a conversation, you should be able to make some connections. Let's unravel what someone has said in its entirety like we would with a problem. When someone talks, they can reveal things like:

1. The topic or subject they are relating to
2. Any beliefs they have
3. What they like or dislike
4. What direction they are moving in
5. Any goals they have
6. What their personality is like
7. Good or bad intentions they have
8. Are they weak or strong?
9. Are they responsible?
10. Are they intelligent?

It's not difficult to figure someone out from a little observation. By looking closely, try to work out what's going on in the mind of a friend, a relative, or a partner. Observe what they talk about, or how they behave by asking yourself some of these analysing questions:

1. What is that person getting at?
2. What are they trying to say?

3. What do they relate to?
4. Are they hinting at something?
5. What's their end game?
6. Is there a purpose in what they say?
7. Do they want something?
8. Are they acting up for a reason?
9. Are they being difficult?
10. Are they showing off to impress someone?

You may need to do a lot a surmising, presuming, and guessing, to make some kind of a connection until you have more information to work with. Once you make enough connections, you will discover what someone's motives are, what their reasons are, any ambitions they have, things they need or want, and the driving force that causes them to say and do as they wish. We are getting to know someone's mentality and psyche. You can't just reveal what someone is feeling and thinking easily unless they tell you. Divulging personal information can lead to a negative impact, so as human beings, we tend not to reveal much to the rest of society. We like to be discreet about what we really think so that we can fit in, function better, and protect our livelihood. New conversations with people can add new pieces to the puzzle. It could take some time until you create a clear picture. So, what should we be listening for, and what other signs could tip us off to what someone is thinking or feeling? Take these observations into account:

1. What are they saying?
2. What aren't they saying?
3. Are they being sarcastic or facetious?
4. What is their tone like?
5. Do they seem distant?
6. Do they trust us?
7. Are they being passive and open-minded?
8. Does that person seem uncomfortable?
9. What is their body language like?
10. Are they deflecting questions?

Act as if you are suspicious, and go over every single word the person in question talks about. Presume that everything revealed is a broad clue to what that person likes, thinks, feels, and wants. Go down the rabbit hole, treating each word and action like we usually would when we solve problems. You should have enough ideas to find those connections. Being incredibly perceptive can be extremely beneficial.

Next, I will show you exactly how to perceive someone that you've just met, and how they will behave in the future. Sound impossible? It's actually straight forward once we have something to work with, and it goes hand-in-hand with what we've just covered. This is about using information we know about someone, to then follow up by elaborating on some key points about what that person does or talks about. We then use logic and our imagination to create extreme circumstances to come up with a theory. It will make more sense as we continue, so take a look at this thought-provoking method:

Importance of perceiving someone

If you want to figure out a new partner within the first few weeks of meeting them, or better still, know how the relationship is going to turn out, you need to look carefully. I have discovered from previous relationships when looking back, that there were clear signs of what my ex-partners' personality was like, any beliefs they had, how they behaved, and a lot more information that could be seen as indicators. If I paid more attention at the time, I would have saved myself years of a wasted life, an avoidance of countless arguments, and be on a completely different path to what I'm on now. It might seem morbid looking for potential character flaws, but its best to know what you are in for before jumping into a relationship. It would be nice to find happiness with someone suitable, but more importantly, it would be beneficial to know if you are making the right decision. It's not based on their social status, are they financially stable, or if they're family making material, it's mainly about how that person is going to treat you, are they mentally sound, and does their lifestyle seem acceptable enough to be a part of. Sharing your life with someone is not something you should rush into unless you don't care how it turns out.

Approach to perceiving someone

Instead of going with the flow no matter how perfect your new date or new partner seems to be, we are going to magnify what that person talks about, and how they behave when we start spending time with them. You should never judge a book by its cover until you have read some of the pages. When meeting someone new, we put on a front because we want the other person to like us, and first impressions can have a lasting impact on how we are judged from things like appearance, posture, and mannerisms. The magic happens within the first few weeks when you get to know that person, and they start to relax, revealing cracks. You will begin to notice small details that might seem irrelevant, but if you magnify what they talk about, or how they behave, no matter how insignificant it seems, you can practically see what's coming. If you looked at your kitchen sides with the naked eye, they would look clean, but if you used a black light in the dark, bacteria would emit a fluorescent glow. I'm not saying your potential partner is full of bacteria; I'm saying you can create a picture from their behaviour, personality, attitude, language, and actions by elaborating on them. More often than not, it's usually a single word or statement that gives away massive clues.

To gain some understanding, I want you to think of a Russian Matryoshka doll, where you have one big wooden doll, and when you open it, there is a smaller doll inside. When you open the smaller doll, there is an even smaller doll inside. This goes on until you end up with a tiny doll. By the time you finish, you have lots of dolls in a line from big to small. Now, let's say you have been dating someone for a few weeks that reveals some negative attributes such as selfishness, ignorance, and a bad temper. Set aside how much you like that person, or how well you get on with them for just a moment. Opening the Matryoshka doll represents a magnification of how bad those attributes could get. Selfishness could lead to being neglected; ignorance could lead to being unloved; a bad temper could lead to an abusive relationship, etc. This might seem farfetched, but what you see on the surface is generally an indication of what's underneath. Earthquake oil set loose above ground indicates there could be an oil field below ground. It's possible for your partner with negative attributes to be full of hot air, meaning its just a front. Make sure you focus on the likely trajectory, whatever they may or may not be. Figuring someone out as early as possible can save time, prevent you from going down the wrong path, and help you make the best decisions before committing to something serious.

How to perceive someone

It's interesting to know that you can make your own intervention before getting too involved. Logic problem solvers shouldn't need telling or warning at any time as long as they are switched on and alert. As I have explained in detail about perceiving someone, take a look at Frank and Sarah's story to make sure that your mindset is where it should be:

- Frank and Sarah have started dating each other, and after three weeks, they begin to feel more comfortable in each other's company. Sarah uses her logic problem-solving skills to work out if a future with Frank, who she is very fond of, is going to lead to something positive. She doesn't care for imperfections; she just wants to be happy. As time went on, Sarah wrote down a few concerns she had in a list:

1. Frank spends a lot of time creating music with his friends. It could be a sign he is neglectful.
2. He seems to call me every time I go out places. I wonder if he's paranoid?
3. Frank seems to go off me when I'm with my best friend, who happens to be male. I hope he's not jealous.
4. He gets angry when he can't think of any new ideas for his music. He's doesn't seem an angry person.

Now that Sarah has something to work with, she looks closer at what this information could signify. All she has to do now is theoretically manifest what Frank could do in extreme circumstances, a bit like a bad dream. Think of it as performing a stress test on a computer graphics card. We need to push it to the limit to see what it's capable of. Sarah needs to expand on what she has seen and heard, by creating a picture of what her future would be like if she started a serious relationship. Instead of trying to create an image of the future, she imagines how bad Frank could progressively get if he continued on the path he's on. That way, she can at least know which direction his behaviour could go in, know what her life with him could be like, and be able to work out if the next few years with him will not be a waste of time. Thinking about the negative possibilities with a kind of forecast instead of being deluded, Sarah decided to stop dating him. She later found out that Frank was more interested in his music rather than friends or family, he had been sacked in the past for hitting his boss, and was known for being a controlling person. Sarah liked him a lot, but instead, she saved herself from being stuck in a potentially harmful relationship.

Look at this from a psychological standpoint on how to evaluate someone before letting them into your life. It's better to shed light on your concerns to make judgements before getting too involved. You can almost see how it will turn out, without waiting for years to find out the hard way. Don't ignore the signs. Have your own interest at heart, and don't feel paranoid by taking precautions. Put your safety, health, and future out of harm's way by avoiding a controlling, abusive, and damaging relationship. Becoming involved with the wrong person can result in endless problems that are not so easy to get out of.

Frank and Sarah's story was about getting personally involved with one another. Here is an example of perceiving people you come into contact with throughout your life:

- Antony wants to befriend Billy at college, and Billy doesn't know who he is, or why he chose him to be a friend. Being smart, Billy keeps his guard up because he doesn't know who he is. Antony could have an agenda or want something from him. We don't like to think bad of people, but there must be a reason motivating Antony to befriend him. He could have good intentions, but we really don't know. These are some of the thoughts going through Billy's head:

1. He wants to be friends and nothing more?
2. He might intend on using me for something bad?
3. Maybe he is attracted to me?
4. He might feel comfortable around me?
5. What if he hangs around me because I'm popular?
6. I could be a decoy for him to get close to one of my friends?
7. I wonder if he's using me to progress or benefit from me?

Later, Antony reveals he has been in prison and has negative views on life. Playing it safe, Billy decides that Antony is not a suitable friend because he has other plans to be successful in life, whereas Antony could lead him to crime. Different circumstances could call for a different decision. If, for example, Billy was writing a book about prison life, it might be ideal for accepting his friendship to listen to Antony's stories. Both of them have to be vigilant because each choice has consequences. As we are only going with our instincts on this occasion, it is important to be realistic about facts when making judgements, instead of using our conscience to justify it. Also, be careful about what you give away to people. Don't let on information about yourself that can be used against you later on. The same goes for actions. Being two steps ahead as a logic problem solver, you are possibly preventing future problems. Think of it as a comfort. Living a calculated life can prevent most problems from happening in the first place, and I say that from experience.

If you find yourself in Billy's or Sarah's situation, the first thing you should do is use the reconnaissance tool. Look out for signs that might indicate what that person is thinking. There are no consequences for trying to work someone out in your head, or for being cautious, so don't feel guilty making presumptions. This tool can be applied to lots of situations. You can use it to figure out what a new boss expects from you, what interest your new friends have, and even what your child will be like when they grow up based on their behaviour, and some of the stuff they say. Maybe you have a young son that hates losing, which could be a sign of being competitive, who then goes on to show an interest in golf, before one day becoming a World Champion. Try it out for yourself and see what results you get.

"All perceiving is also thinking, all reasoning is also intuition, all observation is also invention."

– Rudolf Arnheim

Tool 6. Being resourceful

Being resourceful for logic problem solvers is the ability to find and use available resources to solve problems and achieve goals. Being resourceful is knowing what you need for the results you want in the pursuit of success. To have the right attitude, and to be able to think out-of-the-box in creative ways is the kind of mindset you need, and should have. I'm successful at solving problems, reaching goals, and living the life I want, because the first thing I focus on is finding a weakness, discrepancy, flaw, misconception, or an expectation. I find the gap that has the most importance, then I do what's necessary. Once you have knowledge, then knowledge becomes power, and therefore, there is no reason why you can't overcome boundaries. All of these tools will give you everything you need to become resourceful, dynamic, and versatile. You will be able to demonstrate a willingness to embrace an array of possibilities, opportunities, thoughts, views, suggestions, and experiences outside your sphere. Ascertain a belief that you are capable of resolving any problem. Ask yourself these questions as a guide:

1. Is there another way to get the information I want?
2. Is the desired result going to be enough?
3. Have I looked thoroughly enough?

4. Have I considered everything?
5. Is there anything within the problem I can use for or against, to use to my advantage?
6. Do I know my rights, position, strengths, and weaknesses, etc?
7. Am I using all my surroundings to my advantage?
8. Have I been creative enough with my imagination?
9. Am I efficient enough with the resources I have?
10. Have I been realistic using logic instead of using emotions or my opinion?

There is no better example of resourcefulness than being homeless. It's a huge problem worldwide and can happen to anyone. Experiencing homelessness myself, I've slept in cars, tents, and even in the waiting room at the train station. I've also slept in the snow with a thin jacket, and a bottle of Brandy to keep me warm. At the time, I had no idea what to do once I hit the streets, yet somehow, I was eventually lucky enough to be able to afford a tent and briefly able to sleep in my car; not to mention sofa surfing or the shared houses I've lived in. On some occasions, I roamed the streets with not the first incline on what to do with myself.

Now I'm a logic problem solver, I don't need to wonder anymore what the secrets to surviving homelessness are. I still don't know how to survive on the streets because as far as I'm aware, there is no course to take. Everyone has to fend for themselves. There are charities, food banks, and night shelters, but don't expect much advice from a homeless drunk that can't feel the cold, and couldn't care less where he lays. You need to be able to keep warm, wear the correct clothing, find food and water, and mentally cope on the dark, cold streets for possibly months, even years. Even if you survive outside, the streets can be dangerous. As I wrote this section, four homeless people were sadly murdered in New York as they slept on the streets by a lunatic.

An old friend of mine from high school ended up being homeless as a young man after his mum kicked him out. He was mainly to blame and known for being stubborn, but boy was he resourceful. While some tramps froze to death on benches, he was collecting and selling scrap metal, while sleeping anywhere that was dry and sheltered. Every day, he pushed a shopping trolley around town looking for metal with long hair and scruffy clothes. After some time, he had created a reputation for himself. People gave him unwanted stuff that he would sell on a car boot sale. Shops closing down on the high street let him take the remaining stock worth thousands of pounds. He was making that much money, he was able to rent a warehouse that he filled with junk and metal to sell, while he slept on a mattress in the corner. After ten years on the streets, blowing most of his money on cannabis every day, he eventually rented a house while filling it full of stuff. He had the choice to lead a great life, even start a good business. Because he was receiving so much money, gifts, unwanted items, metal, and doing odd jobs, he would've been worse off leading a normal life. Even to this day, he lives like a tramp. Lewis wasn't just resourceful, he flourished in his stubborn ways without a care in the world. It's a necessity to be resourceful, and some people are better at it than others. Thanks to logic, everyone can work out what they need, and how to obtain it. Take a look at Brad's story and how he applies logic problem solving to his situation. Keep in mind he knows nothing about being on the streets:

- After becoming homeless, Brad finds himself on the streets with nothing other than a change of clothes in his old backpack. With nowhere to go, and without any money, he doesn't know what to do or where to go. He is confused, stressed, and worried, but Instead of letting embarrassment or depression get the better of him, he starts to work out his situation logically. The first thing he does is weigh up his situation as if he came to earth from another planet. He makes a list of priorities to survive after taking into consideration things like the weather, his needs, his safety, and other essentials:

1. Make my way to the town centre where the majority of people go.
2. Find plastic bags to keep my spare clothes completely dry.
3. Ask other homeless people where soup kitchens and charities are located.
4. Try to get a sleeping bag and thick waterproofed clothing from a charity.
5. Search and collect cardboard and newspapers from recycling bins to protect me from the cold floor.
6. Use public toilets in shops to keep clean, and to brush my teeth.
7. Go into café's and food shops to ask if I can do some work in exchange for a meal.
8. Create, build, or find somewhere with a roof above me that is safe enough to sleep out of sight, preferably during the day.
9. Try to keep clean enough to blend in with the general population to avoid being judged, victimised, or discriminated against.
10. Seek shelter when it rains to keep dry, so I don't get sick.
11. Try to get a plastic bottle, and make sure it is filled with water from public toilets.

12. Find somewhere suitable to sleep longterm that will be safe and dry.

Brad comes up with basic ideas for surviving outside in the cold, how to keep watered and fed, and much more using his imagination and logic problem-solving without any help or advice from anyone beforehand. What Brad doesn't do is let things like dignity, pride, emotions, and beliefs get in the way of his resolve. He knows that by using his skills, he will have plenty of jobs to do, and will have plenty to think about instead of concentrating on the dire situation. The fact is, he is in that situation if he likes it or not. His mindset guided and motivated him, giving him a task to complete that saved his life. Within days he had a network of food locations, suitable clothing to wear, and somewhere safe to sleep. People looked down on him, not offering much money as he begged in the town centre. After befriending a homeless drug user that slept half of the day under a doorway, Brad convinced him to take his dog for walks once a day for two hours. Considering the fact that people seemed to care more for the welfare of a dog on the streets, rather than a possible drug user, Brad was given food, money, and dog food, way more than what he usually would've got without the dog. Using his ability to solve problems, within weeks, Brad managed to get a job to earn enough money for a place of his own.

Being resourceful is straightforward when using logic with the tools I have provided. You should at no point run out of ideas as long as you work your way through problems step by step as I have shown you. Do what you must, wait for the right moments, and persevere as you would with any challenge. In this situation, Brad had to become as emotionless as a robot, as smart as a scientist, and as motivated as a bodybuilder. Problems might seem difficult at first, but if you work hard and smart at the beginning, it can really pay off in the long run. If Brad was more concerned about his dignity, rather than finding some waterproof pants, what good would that do him?

"A resourceful person will always make opportunity fit his or her needs." - Napoleon Hill

Tool 7. Visualising ambitions, problems or goals

"You're just not thinking fourth dimensionally," said Emmett Brown in "Back to the Future." Visualising is fun, and can save you time and effort when used with the rest of these tools. It can be used for things like:

- Planning ahead.
- Mentally building a picture.
- Knowing which approach to use.
- Knowing what resources are needed.
- How to keep safe.
- How to act around dangerous people.
- What to do in dangerous situations.
- How to create scenarios.
- How to envision possibilities.
- Prepare for anything unexpected.

I want you to imagine for a second that you are an invisible Hummingbird flying around. Imagine that you can fly through any object, and instantly travel from one location to another anywhere in the World. The next time you have a goal, ambition, or a problem, use your mind to visualise, then focus on what it is you need to do. That way, you can carry out scenarios visually before attempting them in real life. Try to get creative, use your imagination, and of course, use the tools we have covered to make plans, conduct experiments, and decide how you are going to make your approach. Some people don't knowingly visualise unless they need to do a simple task like crossing the road. It has tremendous benefits for planning, predicting, and contemplating. Doing it every day will increase your perception and understanding. The more practice you have, the better you will get. Where the mind goes, the body will follow. In sport, everyone needs to visualise their next move before acting on it.

This tool is great for planning your next course of action. I mainly use it to keep safe. Living in a suburban environment, there are a lot of people, cars, and buildings around me. Growing up with some undesirable friends, I was always visualising consequences from their actions. While my friends got injured or in trouble with the police, I was walking around safe and content. Lots of people have a bad attitude by saying, "you could get hit by a bus tomorrow," or, "you only live once." That's a pretty negative attitude to have when life is a marathon, not a sprint. Things happen when the right conditions are met. Those kinds of people never visualise, because if they did, they would imagine doubt and consequences, and that would stop them from doing stupid things in the first place. As they take life as it comes, and don't really care, they don't see the dangers ahead. I had an old friend that had a stroke and nearly died after crashing his motorbike at high speed, while three other friends on separate occasions were not as lucky. I've met some idiots in my time. It reminds me of people that drive without wearing seatbelts thinking they won't crash, instead of visualising what could happen if they did crash. Anything that can possibly occur should be taken as something that will happen. A bad attitude can get you into heaps of trouble in the long run. Here are five different aspects of visualising to take into account:

Visualising danger

Physically doing simple things in life, such as walking down the road, we can be faced with unknown dangers. For instance, if you wanted to cross the road, and a speeding car was approaching, you would work out if it's safe to cross by measuring the time and distance before the vehicle reached you. If you didn't think there would be enough time to cross, you would wait until it drives past. Another example could be an event that hasn't even happened yet. Let's visualise a truck on a construction site capable of carrying a maximum weight of twenty tons. The tyres can't withstand much more and could explode if any more weight is added. If a tyre was to blow when someone was stood next to it, they could be seriously hurt. By visualising what could happen, it would be wise to stay away from the tyres, especially if someone decides to add more weight. Don't expect to be told, warned, or taught. Don't rely on rules, health & safety, or advice from anyone. Use your initiative with logic to figure things out for yourself.

Visualising a prediction

Predicting what's coming next with high probability, we need to take what we already know or have previously experienced, to determine what might follow next. If you stroke a cat and its tail starts wagging, it could indicate that the cat is annoyed or is in a playful mood. As cats are known to bite and scratch, you can visualise that the cat will attack you if you try to stroke its belly. Before you do, you wear gloves because their teeth and nails are very sharp. We can create a logical argument, then use the conclusion to make an informed decision, but we can also use our senses, experience, knowledge, and wisdom to make a prediction by visualisation.

Visualising a goal

To overcome goals and ambitions, we first need to imagine it. If you can imagine it, you can create it. Visualising will help you work out how to reach that goal. It gives a clear picture of what's possible. Knowing what's needed, you can prepare better by moving in the right direction to succeed. When you contemplate on doing something, you will have probably already visualised it without realising. If you want to live and work in Australia for six months, you will need to imagine what life will be like, where you will live, and what job you could do. It doesn't have to stop there. The more information you know from data, pictures, videos, and maps etc, with a goal in mind, the more you will be able to envision what it will be like on a daily basis. You can work out how you will regularly feel by taking things into account such as the weather, culture, or if there is somewhere to buy the kind of food you like. It all depends on how deep you want go. Cover every aspect, take everything into account, and gather as much information as you can from the start of your goal to the end.

Visualising a problem

Visualising problems with all the other tools we have covered once you utilise them, can give you a good insight into where you need to focus. This is my primary method for working out, planning, countering, and pre-emptively solving problems. Possessing a photographic memory, I learn best when I see things. Tell me someone's name, and I'll forget in seconds. Everyone can visualise a problem; I just do it more than most people. Creating scenarios in your mind can do what reality can't. Envisioning issues in your head once you finish this book, will allow you to test the waters, discover new information, and imagine different possibilities within minutes. You can solve many problems with very little input. Using logic, imagination, and visualisation as a trio, for me, works as a powerful combination. What will your powerful combination of tools be, once you finish reading?

Mental Rehearsal

Mental rehearsal is often done before carrying out an action, as it helps to improve concentration. It also enhances performance and learning. Athletes, for example, visually execute what they're about to do when they kick or throw a ball. Logic problem solvers can use it for working someone or something out, planning or contemplating an action plan, and to visualise what would happen if carried out. We can also visualise the consequences of some actions if we were to carry them out. By gathering as much information as possible, we can understand what we are up against, what we need to do, and when we need to do it.

You should by now understand more about visualising, and all the benefits it has. You might be someone that thinks all the time, or doesn't think enough. I would advise you to visualise as much as possible each time you approach a challenge. Try drawing pictures, diagrams, and writing down anything you think will help you. You could even use maths, do research to support an argument, or envision a series of events to see if it's practical or realistic. Your brain can then become free to deal with the decision-making process. Thinking a lot can make you tired quickly, but if you keep practising, not only will you be familiar with a wide range of subjects, you will be able to think fast and productively. I'm now able to think lightning-fast, toying with scenarios, situations, and problems at my own will without writing anything down. My brain works like a supercomputer. Visualising is freedom that allows you to create a world within your mind that's full of possibilities, and can be used in business, relationships, hobbies, travelling, sport, or to walk up some stairs safely.

"Visualising something organises one's ability to accomplish it." - Stephen R. Covey

Tool 8. Keeping composed

In certain situations, you won't have much time to think fast enough to process any information in your brain when a problem is suddenly upon you. By not being able to think, you are likely to say and do things by mistake, causing more problems. The trick is to keep completely calm and composed to buy enough time to think. The good news is, once you fully understand this book, you will eventually be able to make quick decisions on the spot without needing much time to think under pressure. If an angry driver unexpectedly gets out of his car and confronts you, you would be unable to think or make any decisions because you would be caught off guard. If a thief was to snatch your phone out of your hand, the last thing you might think about is a description of the perpetrator from shock. Just like decisions made in business or sport, it can be very difficult to process information on the spot unexpectedly. When you find yourself in stressful situations, try to answer these three questions. Your mind will no doubt act efficiently with what I have taught you, but if you can, fit these in as you react:

1. What is the opposing person or problem doing at that time?

2. What is the opposing person or problem capable of doing if we don't react?
3. What are the weaknesses of the opposing person or problem?

With sometimes only seconds to react, if the opposing person or problem expands, you contract. If either of them contract, you expand. When there is an opportunity, an opening, a weakness, or the right moment arrives, then you should react logically. When the Russian Spetsnaz (special forces) raid the homes of organised criminals, they enter so fast and hard, that criminals are arrested without a problem. How can anyone possibly react to men abseiling through the living room window like Batman during a game of poker at 4 am with the guys? The reason they entered so abruptly was to prevent the criminals inside from reacting. Unable to think, they didn't try to escape or even attempt to pick up a gun. Not all situations give you time to react. It's the same for accidents, by the time you make sense of what's going on, its already happened. We can, however, do our best to react as logically and as fast as possible, but more to the point, we can predict or prevent most of the problems from happening in the first place.

If a car mounted the curb and headed straight for you, what would you do with the few seconds you have? Most of us would undoubtedly jump out of the way. Some people might freeze on the spot. Some might even presume the driver will stop in time, refusing to move out of the way. As a logic problem solver, you shouldn't make presumptions or use emotions to make decisions. Look at the facts and characteristics of what's going on using logic arguments, then study in detail exactly what's happening from moment to moment. That way, we can use conclusions, connections, measurements, time, considerations, calculations, and anything else to help determine how we should act based on what's about to happen. It might sound like we are trying to solve scientific mysteries, but believe it or not, your brain has rapid processing speed that can process an entire image that the eye sees for as little as 13 milliseconds. Here's how a logical argument would look during a situation within those first few seconds:

- Proposition - a car has mounted the pavement and could run you over.
- Premise - a heavy object on wheels is on a collision course with where you are stood.
- Conclusion - If you stay where you are without moving out of the way, the car will hit you.

Now you have set the standard for important, yet quick questions to establish, you still have unavoidable feelings and emotions to deal with. It's perfectly normal to experience dread, panic and upset, but if you let those emotions take over you during a confrontation, you risk making the wrong judgement, the wrong decision, and performing improper actions. So, what kind of confrontation could happen? Apart from a car mounting the pavement, an argument could develop between yourself and another person in a nightclub. Countries have confrontations all the time, sometimes leading to war. I was once chased by a Rottweiler dog, giving me seconds to decide what to do. If you are known for keeping cool under pressure, then great; just don't forget to use all of your abilities for the best approach. If you are terrified by confrontation like me, it's best to understand what you feel so you can manage your emotions better during the fight or flight response. Keeping composed is key to being able to think clearly. Speaking in front of large audiences can give someone stage fright. The body is overcome by fear and anxiety, preventing them from thinking straight. Bullies torment their victims by prompting them to say or do things they wouldn't naturally, then they distract them from thinking so that the victims make fools of themselves. Sometimes, the only thing you can do is go with the flow to deflect problems.

Stress is the body's reaction to change that requires an adjustment or a response. The body then reacts with physical, mental, and emotional responses. You can experience stress from your environment, your thoughts, and even from positive life changes such as a promotion, a mortgage, or the birth of a child. Swap fear with anticipation; worry with concern; dread with caution. Personally, since becoming a logic problem solver, I see every confrontation as a challenge; just don't overthink like me. If you have a deadline for work or university, take one step at a time. By reacting calmly and composed in situations, half of the battle is already won. Fight back emotions to be able to think collectively. As long as you have time to think in a controlled state of mind, you will be able to apply everything from this book. The weakness logic problem solvers have is time, or not having the right conditions to think clearly. Don't be defeated by temporary feelings.

Before moving on to the next tool, make sure you have an understanding, by adopting the right mindset for critical thinking. As we have just covered stress, we shall stop for a moment to make sure that you are taking all of this in. Stress is considered a problem, so like problems, we need to understand, reflect on, and work through it to know how it affects us? If the information below doesn't relate to what you should be thinking, then you are not thinking along the right lines. Don't worry though, it will all make sense by the time you reach the end of this book. So, here goes. What are the characteristics of stress, and what's our thesis:

1. We can't think clearly to make good decisions because of stress.
2. Stress presents itself as a problem, so we ask, "what is stress?"
3. By doing research, we know the premise of stress.
4. We now know how the human body reacts in certain situations.
5. We need to dig deeper because the problem leads to other issues like anxiety.
6. The information can be used to understand what's happening to our body.
7. By understanding the root cause of the problem, we can find a way to manage it.
8. After finding a way to manage it, we can conclude that it's not a problem anymore.
9. Because it's not a problem, we can think more clearly under pressure or during a confrontation.

These results solve four things:

1. You have a better understanding, even if you don't wish to act.
2. You know how to overcome the problem if you choose to or not.
3. You are equipped with information and knowledge that you might not have had before.
4. You have added a new solved problem to your list that can be used for future reference.

You should now be aware of how important it is to keep calm under pressure. Don't forget to ask yourself priority questions at the start, to identify what's happening. Understanding is valuable for making the right decision, whereas in the past, you might have struggled to comprehend what the heck is going on.

"It's about being smart, taking your time, keeping your composure, just going out there and being the best that you can be." - Floyd Mayweather, Jr.

Tool 9. Asking the right questions

Using this tool will help you to ask the right questions when faced with a problem or a challenge, which will lead to the correct answers. You will find that there is always a connection once you reveal a reason or a cause to a problem. Do you remember being a kid asking your parents questions, then following up with "why" after every sentence; this is precisely the same. If you presume or accept that things just happen in life, then think again. Even if situations are in our favour, we can't deny the fact that something is tipping the balance to our advantage, just like you can't be ignorant or narrow-minded to what's going on around you. To be able to ask the right questions, make sure you are not asking them based on what you believe to be true, or because of your old mindset. Ask questions based on logic. This is simply a means to an end, logic over illogical, and facts over fiction. Ask questions that follow suit; it helps to create a picture with answers that we can work with. Using the process of reasoning with backward induction as we often do, we can start with the conclusion to know exactly what to aim for. You can do this for goals, problems, and situations. It can help you figure out a lot of stuff that you don't understand in life. Take a look at this interview by Louise, who wants to know how Martha created a successful blog:

Martha runs a blog that earns her $10.000 every month! Louise wants to know how she became so successful by asking some questions. What Martha doesn't know is that Louise is a logic problem solver. Being prepared, Louise focusses on very specific and targeted questions to find out exactly what she needs to know:

Q: How did you make a blog?

A: I researched online for two weeks until I had enough information.

Q: How did you get so much traffic?

A: It was slow for a few months, but then I started to get organic traffic from Google by writing content based on a specific niche. I also started a Facebook page where I could post content. Because I had some funny pictures relating to my blog, I got loads of shares from paid advertising directly from Facebook. Some of it went viral, which brought tons more people to my blog.

Q: What did you write about, where did you find it, and why was it so popular?

A: I wrote about dieting that saved money, but made people feel full instead of feeling hungry or dizzy. I searched forums like Reddit and looked on Amazon to see what their bestselling books were. By finding something that people talked about, and wanted, I knew my blog would be popular.

Q: How did you make money from it?

A: Once I got a few thousand visitors each month, I was able to activate Google AdSense. The second monetisation method was to post affiliate products on my blog. There is plenty of other ways as well.

Q: What's AdSense?

A: Adsense is advertising from Google. If I place the ads on my blog or website, every time someone clicks on an ad, I get a small commission.

Q: How much do you get?

A: It varies, but the more traffic you have, you more money you make; anything from a few hundred dollars to a few thousand.

Q: What's an affiliate product?

A: I went on Clickbank to search for a weight loss course, then promoted it on my blog. Every time someone bought the course, I got a commission of up to 50%.

Q: What made you decide to create a blog?

A: I wanted to make money from home while I look after three kids, and I know how hard it is to lose weight, so it became a passion of mine. Helping people gives me satisfaction. The most important part is keeping people engaged.

Louise was determined to find out how to start a successful blog, so she asked the right questions. She started with a conclusion, then worked her way backwards until she found the premise and proposition. Louise did everything she could to obtain the correct information. By asking particular questions to get to the root cause, she received valuable answers. It's important to concentrate on the key points. Ask indirect questions, and you might lead yourself to wrong conclusions. If you can't find an answer to a question, don't give up. You will be met with constant barriers, even if you have solutions. You will get to a point where there are no more questions that need asking. Logic problem solvers are relentless, and they don't quit.

"To ask the right question is already half the solution of a problem." - C.G. Jung

Tool 10. Answering questions correctly

Answering a question wrong could be the direct cause of a problem depending on the nature of a conversation. We could refuse to answer by ignoring someone, but that would indicate we are not cooperating. If I'm asked a question, the first thing I think about is what that person wants. It can be hard being vigilant all the time. Naturally, we are social beings, so we like to talk. How harmless can a conversation be you might be wondering? Words can be used as weapons against us. To work out why a question is being asked, we can use backward induction as we often do. A friend might want to know what plans you have on a particular day. An awkward question could come from your boss about incomplete work. Another bunch of questions could arise from your husband, who is blaming you for something you didn't do. How you answer will have consequences, but before you say a word, wonder if there is an agenda involved? Decide if there's a motive for what's being asked? Always think before replying. People generally want something, even if its good or bad. Your answers could cause issues, friction, implications, and in some circumstances incriminate you.

As a logic problem solver, if you wish to avert a problem from materialising, its best to answer carefully. Being cautiously perceptive, I am always ten steps ahead. I can determine the outcome of the conversation by answering the opposite of what that person was expecting me to say, because I can see what they are getting at, what they are implying, or how they might be influencing me. Unfortunately, being pessimistic in this day and age seems to help for established reasons behind the scenes. Even if someone is trying to make small-talk, you should always ponder with suspicion. People could use your answer to benefit themselves, act maliciously against you, or if you're lucky, take an interest in you because you appeal to them. Knowledge is power. If someone is gathering information that could affect you in some way, you can prevent it with your choice of words before answering. I'm not telling you to lie or to be dishonest; I'm just telling you to be careful with what you say. Your judgement comes down to your beliefs, your senses, and your instincts. The next time someone asks you a question, determine what they could do with that information? So, how can we answer correctly in future? What questions need answering, and which don't? Here are two examples of the pitfalls:

- Your friend calls you up one day to ask what you are doing on Tuesday, at 6 pm. You quickly presume in your mind that they want you to babysit. The reason you came to that conclusion is that you know they like to go to bingo once a week. You respond by telling your friend that you might be busy. That way, you can find out what they want while staying neutral. You can see if an offer benefits you without being rude by keeping your options open. As it turns out, she wanted you to babysit as suspected. If you were to say "no," it might cause problems with your friend after all the times they have helped you out. You prevented a potential problem without being awkward at the same time.

- Betty sits down in her living room just as the phone rings. When she answers, a man claims to be a Police officer. He explains that she has been a victim of fraud. Shocked by the news, she is then told that the Police officer needs her bank card details to stop any more money from being taken out. Unfortunately, Betty is old, has no reason not to believe him, and doesn't want to lose any more money, so she gives him her card details. The man later emptied her bank account in a scam. Although Betty was vulnerable, she should have called her bank to confirm that money has been taken out. You should always stop to think before answering, no matter what kind of pressure you're under. You should always do your due diligence by researching, confirming, and verifying what's being said. Scams can happen to anyone. You should pay more attention when doing the things you're familiar with as opposed to doing something unfamiliar. You may not know it, but we are most susceptible when we are doing stuff that's expected. Having a sense of trust in friends, family, or in our own actions, we tend to become passive without a need to question ourselves, or the people around us.

Questioning is the ability to organise our thinking around what we don't know. Take someone's position into consideration. Are they an authority? Do they have power? Do they have influence? Whatever you say could have serious implications. Nobody likes to judge or think the worst of people, but if you stay vigilant, then you won't fall into any problems blindly. A friend might ask you to play tennis. Even though it's fun and benefits you, a sentence or phrase was used to find out information. How you answer is entirely up to you. It can be like a double-edged sword; on the one hand, you could be trusting, open, and easy-going, and on the other hand you could land yourself in trouble, expose yourself, or become a target.

Sometimes a problem can only be solved once questions are answered. This could be an opportunity to demonstrate your skills. Colleagues, friends or family might need help answering a question to figure out a problem. When that happens, you could show off by logically working it out. Watch everyone marvel at your findings, and your ability to find the connections, before arriving at a conclusion. Armed with knowledge, a proper mindset, and a better perception than most, you will get results far better than anyone else.

"Sometimes the questions are complicated and the answers are simple." - Dr. Seuss

Well done for getting this far! You might be thinking that you understand everything up to this point, which is excellent but don't rush off just yet. Show me you have the patience of a disciplined logic problem solver by reading to the end!

Tool 11. Everything happens for a reason

Everything happens for a reason, no, seriously, and I don't mean spiritually, or your unforeseen destiny that you believe will reveal itself. There is a logical explanation for almost everything that happens in life. When things go wrong, people reassure themselves by saying, "everything happens for a reason." That might help you get through a crisis, and you can hold on to your faith by all means, but let's look at how there is a connection between everything we see and do. Have you ever wondered why the tide goes in and out, or why men get paid more than women? When we use backward induction, we can figure out what's happening, and why. I need you to be able to see things for what they really are, but I can only do that so long as you're not stuck in your old ways, with your own beliefs. It's hard for some people to change their stance over a matter when they believe they are correct. You can't teach an old dog new tricks; or can you? I know people don't like change, but unless you're open to other possibilities, how can you expect to question the integrity of someone else? If you were told that the vehicle you were buying had no problems, would you believe them? What's presented before you might not be what it seems, but let's go over that in just a moment. Read this story about a man that wouldn't change his stance on what he thought to be true:

- An old man builds a spec house for his daughter during his retirement. Being in the building trade for over forty years, he claims to know what he is doing from experience. An argument unfolds between him and his daughter because she believes he might have used the wrong wood. Adamant he's been using the same wood throughout his career, he refuses to listen to anyone's opinion, because he believes that his long service in the trade outweighs what anyone else has to say. After an official inspection, it turned out that he had used the wrong wood under health and safety regulations that changed two years prior. They had to start over losing a lot of money. Not caring for what anyone was telling him, and looking stupid as well as being wrong, the old man gets angrier by refusing to admit he was wrong in the first place. Unfortunately, his pride and beliefs got the better of him. Life does not need your permission; it knows how to evolve without your consent.

Now you are becoming more of a passive thinker, let's see why things happen for a reason, and in what sense is there a connection. Stop taking things on face value. There is generally a motivation, a purpose, or an objective for how something operates, why people say and do the things they do, and why life is the way it is. Logically work your way backwards with what you decide to focus on by analysing, investigating, and questioning the world around you. Look at these examples to see how there's more than meets the eye:

- My friend in the UK bought a shirt online from the US costing $20, and the delivery cost $30. He was angered because the UK post office was charging him an additional postage fee on arrival. Without thinking too much into it like most people, he didn't stop to think of anything other than the charge. He mentioned how the postage costed more than the t-shirt, yet he didn't care to explore why. I explained to him that the seller would increase the postage cost to make more profit. It didn't seem plausible for the postage to cost $30 when the package was small and light. In my opinion, it would cost no more than $10-$15. After doing some research, the postage for a small package was $12 or lower for something as light as a t-shirt. We don't know if the seller did this to make profit intentionally, but the fact is, the seller will make around $40 profit.

You can start with a presumption, information already known, or information that has been researched. Putting everything into question, we can reveal and uncover what's behind the scenes, regardless of any excuses, coincidences, or justifications. We can find out or come close to how something operates. Even if you don't get the answers you want, you will gain an understanding which can be valuable for future decisions. All you have to do is reach for that inner child by asking "why" all the time, for whatever you want to know, something you are unsure or unfamiliar about, or something that seems suspicious. You don't even need a reason. The advantage you gain from critical thinking is that over time, your awareness and understanding will dramatically increase. Not only is this fun, but it will also turn you into an excellent logic problem solver from your curiosity alone. Here is another example:

- Every time I go on YouTube, I notice that a lot of the thumbnail images are fake, and the title is often an exaggerated lie. By displaying false information, millions of people click on the video like a moth to a lightbulb. The thumbnail will show something ridiculous, like a gigantic hole in the sea, or two people facing each other that weren't alive at the same time. After forgetting why they clicked on it in the first place, the viewers end up being duped into watching a stupid video. Photoshopped images are made to convince people to click on the video without a single thought. By gaining thousands, even millions of views, the video creator makes a lot of money. The thumbnail is nowhere to be seen in the video because it doesn't exist. I can't help but think that millions of people have unknowingly clicked on a video, making the creator thousands of dollars. It's the same about your privacy when you go on a website; you have no idea what data they are harvesting from you because you didn't read their privacy policy. Don't do something blindly without knowing why it's there in the first place. Even though we can't always be sure, we can't deny the facts. We might be considered to be judgemental, pessimistic, even cynical, but you never know when critical thinking could protect you or benefit you in the future. Times frequently change, and so should you. "You can't kid a kidder," as my grandad used to say. Put everything you have ever known into question, then see what results you get.

So, why does any of this have anything to do with problem-solving? Because what you see and believe might not be entirely accurate, and as you make decisions based on what you believe to be true, you could end up doing something wrong, something you regret, or fall into a trap that could cause lots of other problems.

"When I see a bird that walks like a duck and swims like a duck and quacks like a duck, I call that bird a duck."
- James Whitcomb Riley

Tool 12. Preparation & Pre-emptive action

Being prepared or pre-emptively taking action beforehand can be the difference between success and failure. Problems can start small, giving us time to prepare. They can also come expected or unexpected. Once a problem seems to form, or whether it's already happened, it will generally sit there until you fix it, or until enough time has passed to render it insignificant which could be a very long time. Sometimes a problem needs to be solved within a certain amount of time. Whatever time you have, it's important to use it to your advantage. It's good to nip it in the bud to prevent it from getting worse, but it's even better when you prepare yourself with the tools and knowledge before the problem happens. Wherever the problem came from, or even if you brought it on yourself, you have to treat the root cause as an opposition, and as an opposition, it's against what you are trying to achieve. Every problem must be approached as a challenge using no emotions, no judgement, and without getting personally involved. You need to make logical and calculated decisions that benefit you. Every decision needs to be an improvement, an advancement, or an advantage in your favour. Your mindset should be that of an athlete; nothing other than winning using any means necessary matters. Fail to recognise that, and you risk being defeated. There has to be a motivation for logically working through issues.

I've been torn between emotions of what's right and wrong in the past. The reality is, if you don't make decisions that benefit you, in the end, you are going to suffer at the hands of people, companies, law, relationships, enemies, the environment, and anything else capable of generating a problem. We all make mistakes, and most problems in life are from our own doing. When that happens, we must challenge ourselves as we would anyone else. The worst dilemma you will face is being emotionally involved with people you care about. What we 'want' to do can sometimes counteract with what we 'should' do. In the end, the choice is entirely down to you. Will you go with your heart? Or will you use your head?

Let's start with preparing for a problem. First of all, measure how much time you have to solve your issue. You might want to use the reconnaissance tool and a few others before making a plan. Know what you are dealing with before taking any steps. If you use the tools I have shown you, you should have an idea of what to expect. If someone is trying to sue you, learn what your rights are. If a chain of events is knowingly going to happen, do everything you can to prepare using your logic problem-solving abilities. There are only so many precautions we can take to prevent problems; naturally, they will happen regardless. Visualise and plan a step by step process on how you're going to solve it. Battle through those emotions and feelings, pulling you backwards and forwards in a tug-of-war. Prepare for things you need to say, do, and act upon, that will place you in a strong position. Aim for the best outcome, and be willing to do what it takes to reach it. You will also find that the situation is not as bad as you first thought. Study, analyse and know exactly where the problem is coming from, and why it's happening. You can never be too prepared.

One method that is more powerful than preparing is pre-emptive action. This is by far one of the most valuable tools in this book. How would you feel if you had the power to deflect a problem, stop it in its tracks, or prevent it from happening in the first place? This is not something you might think about because most people live from moment to moment. To do this, we need to prepare, research, plan, position ourselves, and put things into place. First, work out where the problem is, what the problem is trying to achieve, and what's your ideal outcome. It's all about knowing what's about to happen. Take what you already know, or can find out, add that to what you don't want to happen, or would like to happen, then find a weakness or a discrepancy that invalidates the root cause of the problem, so that we can pre-emptively act beforehand. You are taking pervasive action by putting things in place before the problem materialises. There is never any certainty, however, if a problem takes shape, who knows how bad it will become. By learning what we have covered, you should easily be able to prevent problems. You could consider this as crafty or cunning on the face of it, but all we are doing is engineering the outcome in our favour, and that's why this tool has to be my favourite. Use it for good purposes, then reap the rewards.

I don't advise you to create problems using pre-emptive action unless it's for a good cause. Animal conservationist, for example, will cut the horns off Rhino's to prevent poachers from killing them. It will grow back like a nail and is painless, but still a necessary evil to prevent them from becoming extinct. As I've been explaining, focus on the outcome you want. Only then can you take the steps you need. The main principle for logic problem solving is starting at the end, destination, or conclusion, then working your way backwards. You can't order a takeaway unless you know what you want to eat.

Look at these three examples below. The first is about a problem we can expect, the second is about a problem we don't expect, and the third example is about pre-emptively acting before a problem begins:

1. Kim watches the news to find that a storm is on its way. Gale force winds and snow is expected over the next two days. The snow could make the ground treacherously

slippy with below-freezing temperatures. The wind is expected to damage property with a risk to human life. It's bad news for Kim because her house is on a hill. To get into her home, she has to walk up some steps or drive up her sloping driveway. With snow and ice on the way, she could have an accident, so she plans on buying plenty of cat litter for her steps. The second problem is her art sculpture in the back garden. Not expecting lousy weather for at least another month, she has to make arrangements to get it moved. If she doesn't, all of her hard work will get destroyed by the weather, and that's an issue because she makes a living from creating custom made sculptures. By pre-emptively taking action beforehand, she puts things in place to avert a problem from ever happening. This might seem like common sense, but there is plenty of room to get creative for any problem you have.

2. I was driving with my Uncle one day when we started to approach a round-a-bout. We had the right of way, so my Uncle drove on to the round-a-bout to turn right. From our left, a car had carried on driving without stopping, heading straight towards where I was sat. As a logic problem solver, I anticipated that the driver might not stop. My Uncle was looking to his right, so after quickly alerting him, he came to a halt before we collided. After his road rage with horn beeps and swearing, he was angry

because the car on our left should've given way to us. I explained to him not to expect other drivers to abide by the rules. Even though the driver should've given way, he still had his own will to do whatever he wanted. I told my Uncle to look at what people 'could' do instead of what they 'should' do. If I weren't with him that day, he would have crashed. Never presume anything, yet question everything.

3. Sometime before 2014, the US infiltrated the Cuban hip-hop scene to spark youth unrest. It was an attempt to unseat Cuba's communist government. America has a strategy to stop communism from spreading throughout the world, just take a look at the Cold War with the Soviet Union, and the Vietnam War. Like previous efforts including exploding cigars, Cuban Twitter, and the botched Bay of Pigs Invasion, the attempt to co-opt rappers ended in epic failure. For more than two years, US Aid had secretly been trying to infiltrate Cuba's underground hip-hop scene. Their elaborate plan to "break the information blockade," was to use Cuba's rappers to build a network of young people who would go on to spark a movement against the government of President Raul Castro. Aldo, a rap artist, along with his group known as Los Aldeanos, were known for lyrically protesting against the Castro government's grip on

everyday life. They ended up getting sucked into a tug-of-war between Washington and Havana. The US thought they could use the rap groups influence to spread democracy through lyrical songs. Executed by amateurs, the operation failed to start a democratic revolution after being compromised. We can see that the communist government was the problem, and the US wanted to solve that problem by pre-emptively putting something in place to gain an advantage. It may be a little farfetched for solving issues in our daily lives, but I'm sure you get the gist of it. What was your opinion on the US using a hip-hop group to create an uprising? Do you think it was clever or cunning?

Putting things in place is something you already do without realising. You might tighten loose floorboards at home in case someone trips up. You also might tell a friend about your new plans for that evening. Instead of approaching problems directly, see if you can put something in place beforehand. Try to pick up warning signals, or look at the big picture with awareness to your surroundings. Being prepared, organised, and ready can be all that's needed sometimes.

"The best preparation for tomorrow is doing your best today." - H. Jackson Brown, Jr.

Tool 13. Logic Expectations

Logic expectation is about looking at your environment in detail, separating every entity you see, then deciding what can be used to aid you. In essence, we are using the environment to our advantage. The next time you go outside, take a good look around. Cars drive in specific directions because they are being driven forward. People walk down the street by putting one step in front of another. We can make plans based on what we expect to be logically valid. We also need to think of every possibility by finding connections. To be able to assess situations, make better decisions, or predict a likelihood, we separate everything we see, look where it originates from, learn what it's capable of, and also learn what its purpose is. Don't ignore the garbage truck you see every week, look at why it's there, where it's going, and what part it plays in everyday life. Ask yourself if any external factors could disrupt what we expect. Use your environment to assist you, but always respect it. Whenever there is a new development, you need to reassess the situation all over again. It might seem daunting, but changes can happen every second, every hour, or every week, etc. To explain more clearly, take a look below at Beth's story, and how she needs to create a movie scene for College:

Beth needs to create a scene about a desperate father, who intends on robbing a bank to pay for the release of his daughter, that's been kidnapped. The robbery needs to be successful, or his daughter will get hurt. To make the scene realistic, Beth needs to take everything into account. Using her logic problem-solving skills, she intends on using her entire surroundings to her advantage. She simplifies every entity based on its purpose, where it will be, and when it will be there. Before narrowing it down, she thinks about intricate details such as measurements, time, possibilities, geography, routines, expectations and much more. It helps when she slows everything down, writes it down on paper, then makes a plan. Think of it as a recipe, the better ingredients you have, the more sophisticated the results will be. Turn your brain into a computer by harvesting as much knowledge, information, and data as possible.

Logically working through her plan, Beth starts with the end result, which is the robbery itself. Following the connections backwards, she begins to create a picture turning distinct information into a guiding lighthouse. These are some of the associations she finds to create a picture:

- What's a robbery? It's a crime. What happens if a crime is committed? The police will come.

- What are the police capable of? They have good communication, they come in numbers, and they have access to cars, motorbikes, boats, helicopters, guns, tasers, dogs, and more.
- How will the police respond? There are roads and an open sky, so mainly by car and helicopter.
- Will a police officer respond if he feels tired? Because he has a duty, he is expected to respond.
- What's the protocol for the police answering a call? After doing some research, we learn they need to assess the situation by attending.

To some people, this might look as if we are stating the obvious, when in fact, we intend on using this information to make a watertight plan based on what's expected. Irrelevant information that has no purpose can be discarded. What kind of underwear the police are wearing does not affect our situation, and doesn't need to be taken into account. Miscellaneous details on whether the police radios will work is also irrelevant, because we must presume they are in working order unless communications were somehow disabled. Making a plan of your own might tick some of the boxes that counteract with expected consequences, but that doesn't mean it will work unless you get lucky. For the highest success rate after any unexpected possibilities, your best chance is to cover every expectation you can find.

Beth needs to know very particular information by finding connections, to then form arguments? Now she has some data, Beth can start making conclusions. She views this information as an opposition, that's trying to prevent her character from carrying out a successful bank robbery. If her character, the desperate father, attempts to rob the bank, he will be met by an organisation (the law) that will stop him. Beth now needs to make a plan that will counter any opposition. Because the father needs to pay the ransom as soon as possible, she needs to focus on creating a fast bank robbery. Beth creates a hypothesis based on expectations that she has researched, to then use in different scenarios:

- Every consequence from every action needs to be placed in a timeline. If the father tries to stick-up the bank, someone could alert the police. If they are alerted, they will try to attend as fast as possible to investigate, mainly by car using the roads. Because that is now a fact or a strong possibility, the roads have become the main focus to intercept, and obstructing the police is now a priority. Imagination comes into play to block, divert, or obstruct the roads. This can be done using fake road works, pretending a lorry has broken down, creating a makeshift roadblock, and even staging a fight in the middle of the road. There will be a lot of routes to and from the bank, so maybe spotters could keep a lookout as well. To do any of this, the father will need resources and manpower to assist him. What if the police helicopter gets called? The helicopter is just another resource for the police, and if that resource has already been used up for another incident, it can't respond. By staging a missing person with dementia that has wondered off into some woods far away from the bank, more time has been bought. Beth also needs to make sure that the father won't be trapped inside the bank by the security doors, along with other precise details.

After methodically making the perfect plan, the bank robbery was successful, and Beth's movie scene was a roaring success. You should now be one more step closer to becoming a productive logic problem solver; just don't go robbing banks! You should now be thinking along the right lines. It's not always easy covering every aspect. Obstacles in life will continue to challenge you. Make good use of these skills, and you will see tremendous benefits if patient. The more you practice, the sooner you will change your mindset by re-wiring your brain. There is never a guaranteed solution to a problem. You have to take into account unexpected changes, different circumstances, and human behaviour that could change moment to moment. Fortunately for you and me, nobody will know what we are capable of, or the resolve we have when met with challenges.

Flipping a coin to what we have just covered about logic expectations, the people around you that know you on a personal level will have their own perception and expectations. They can use that knowledge against you to cause problems. Having a personality, ambitions, and intentions, we give away signals and vibes that people pick up on to make decisions against us. You don't have to become a recluse like me, just don't give much away. Think carefully before speaking. Lead a more private life if you can. Become unpredictable instead of being someone that your friends and peers know too well. If you have habits, attachments, obsessions, or routines, they could be used against you by those with bad intentions. Be careful who you show weakness to when you are sick, or in a bad position. Know your strengths and weaknesses, and always be vigilant. You need to presume that the one person you think you can trust forever, might one day turn on you. Don't be taken for a fool due to your good nature to help people. During a lifetime, you will encounter jealousy, betrayal, competition, bullies, lies, greed, incompetence, and many other factors that will cause you nothing but sleepless nights. Give someone an inch, and they will take a mile.

Use logic at all times. What I don't want you to do, ever, is guess, presume, or believe you know what will happen. You can though, use other forms of logic if you wish. It's essential to see beyond what's going on and to identify what could be a problem. If there are pieces to the puzzle missing, you will make bad decisions. Smaller obstacles need to be overcome until there are no more problems. The number of issues you encounter could be vast, the time it takes could be years, and the possibilities could be endless.

"It is easy to be wise after the event."
- Arthur Conan Doyle

Tool 14. It's all in the detail

In this tool, we're going to look at the smaller details in life, the sort of things you might not pay attention to like, body language, speech, or someone's behaviour. Observing small details gives off valuable information. Think about psychology, and how it can be used to work out what someone could be thinking, feeling, or contemplating. Indications of someone's intentions might not be so easy to obtain, but if we were to study their body language, we might be able to read into them. It might be hard to observe your surroundings with the fast, productive lives we live, but if you pay more attention, slow things down a little, and watch what's going on around you, you will notice work colleagues flirting, a teenage boy resting his fist against his cheek because he's bored, or a passenger on the bus purposely placing their bags on the seat next to them, to prevent anyone from sitting down. Any information gathered can help you make decisions without a single word being spoken. You can use knowledge to avoid, divert, or solve problems. Logic problem solving is about tipping the balance in our favour. Starting with the basics below, let's study body language, speech, and behaviour to raise your perception skills. I've even added a thought-provoking bonus that might be useful.

Body Language

When people don't express their thoughts verbally, they still throw off clues to what they are thinking and feeling. Keep an eye out for non-verbal messages communicated through body movement and facial expressions. Crossed arms and legs suggest defensiveness, anger or self-protection. When people place their hands in their pockets or put them behind their back, it suggests that they are hiding something. Our eyes also give away a lot of information based on what's going on in the brain. Body language is not as apparent as talking. Interpreting someone plays a big part in how we interact with them. It's a silent dance of micro expressions, hand gestures, and posture that registers in the brain immediately, even when we are not consciously aware of them. However brief an interaction last, it can still have long-lasting repercussions to how an individual interprets someone's motivation, mood, and openness. It makes us wonder how we are also perceived. If you are in a problematic situation that involves people, pay close attention to them. You can pick up clues from gestures, eye contact, touch, space and voice. I've always studied body language from a young age. Because I was a small kid that grew up in a bad neighbourhood, it was important to fit in without becoming a target. Taking in my surroundings, I learnt from observing body language how to behave, how to blend in, and when to speak. Trying to avoid problems growing up, I felt I had to portray a particular image. Not because I wanted to, but because it was necessary to avoid being a target. I chose to be under the wing of a dragon instead of being on the receiving end. Sometimes, the only way to solve or avoid problems is by doing the things we don't want to.

Verbal communication

When a person talks, just like body language, we can work out what they are thinking and feeling, along with any intentions they have. There is a meaning, and a purpose behind every word said to us. If there were no meaning, everyone would be talking gibberish all the time. Even when a friend is talking about crap, they are revealing information. So, what exactly do we need to keep an eye out for? Firstly, soak up everything you hear like a sponge from conversations, comments, or what's being said about you. By doing so, we can discover what someone's intentions are, how they emotionally feel, and what kind of stuff they think about. People hide behind egos, personas, fake personalities, and also behind an image to protect their interest. It's possible to seek out if they have good or bad intentions towards us. From a single comment, we can work out how much someone likes us, and we can also sense danger. The more you know about an individual's background and personality, the better conclusion you will come up with, and that is precisely what you need to make better decisions. As human beings, we can be:

1. Worshipped
2. Tricked
3. Lied to
4. Misguided
5. Supported
6. Distracted
7. Directed
8. Bullied
9. Cherished
10. Scammed
11. Taught
12. Influenced, and more.

Words are powerful, so don't take them lightly. Listen out for those who trip themselves up, by giving away clues to what they think. When someone is drunk, they tend to tell the truth by revealing information they wouldn't usually talk about if they were sober. Reflect on previous conversations that you had an hour earlier; you will be surprised at what you can pick up on. Watch and listen like a hawk for things like sarcasm, changing the subject, distractions, whispering, false information, being misguided, and kept out of discussions.

If you think someone is about to cause you problems, don't act irrationally, instead, ask the person what they mean or what they are implying. If that person notices you have become aware of their true nature, they will go back into their shell, and you won't reveal much. Don't make the mistake of getting information wrong, or you could suffer in the long run. Don't accuse people by pointing the finger without knowing the full picture. It's also a good idea to remember, write down, or record what has been said. Words have a tendency of coming back to haunt you. Recording a conversation on your phone discretely could be used for reassurance as a pre-emptive action. If you do things correctly and above water, you won't need to worry because those who create problems will soon be eating their own words. Don't take any prisoners by feeling bad or paranoid; words can obliterate a person's life and reputation. We can also be left vulnerable from our own words, so be careful with what you say, and who you say it to. If you were to tell one person a secret, you might as well tell the whole world. One person knowing tells someone else, then that person tells another;

before you know it, everyone knows your business. Trust is only as good as it last. Loose lips sink ships.

Behaviour

Behaviour can give away just as much information as body language and verbal communication, if not more. Good intentions can cause problems just as much as bad ones. Take notice of what someone starts doing, or doesn't do. Their collection of behaviour, what they talk about, and body language can give an insight into what's going on in that person's head. Actions speak louder than words. Read this story about studying someone before they act:

- Hours after getting back from a weekend away, Susan overheard her parents arguing. The three of them stayed in a lake house two hours away from their home. Her dad was angry because he left his laptop back at the lake house, and he needed it for work. Susan wanted to help her dad but knew her parents wouldn't allow it. Her idea was to sneak out of the house, go to the bus station, then jump on a bus to get her dad's laptop. It was dangerous because she was only fourteen and wasn't accompanied by an adult. Believing she was doing the right thing, Susan started to prepare for the trip. Her mother grew suspicious after noticing things around the house. The first thing she noticed was the mess on the kitchen side after someone had made a sandwich. She became further suspicious when Susan asked how frequent the busses were. After keeping an eye out, her mother heard a noise coming from Susan's bedroom, so she quickly ran in. Susan had smashed open her piggy bank, taken her savings, and was trying to climb out of the window before her mum stopped her. She thought she would make her dad happy by going back to the lake house for his laptop. Her mother noticed how her behaviour had become suspicious before she tried to carry out her plan. Instead of one problem, there could have been two problems. Using her intuition, awareness, and a keen eye, her mother was able to notice the warning signs.

The same can be considered for someone that has bad intentions towards us. If you start to notice behaviour that seems negative, then go with your gut by taking it seriously. Where there is smoke, there is fire. You could wrongly portray someone, but sometimes it's better to be safe than sorry. Don't rely heavily on trust or presumptions. People never cease to amaze. Keep your enemies close and your friends closer, because it's your friends that are in a position to do more damage than what your enemies could do.

Mimicking

Entirely your choice while I'm on the subject, but there is a useful unorthodox behaviour that's given me profound success when dealing with people. It is similar to mimicking, but instead, it's more about blending in by acting how another person would expect us to act. Let's say you want to impress your boss or deflect verbal abuse during an angry confrontation; you could naturally be yourself by reacting how you usually would, risking a negative response, or, you could act in a way that gives you an advantage. Study how the other person behaves from the second you meet them. Use their position or stance to act accordingly to what they would deem as acceptable, appealing, positive, or promising. Think of it as placing a mirror in front of them. It's not about kissing someone's butt; it's more of a fast track to fitting in as soon as possible. By doing this, you can convey to people that you are on the same level, you're committed, suitable, and on the same team as them. Just like attending an interview; you dress to impress. This is perfect for the times when you don't know how to act. Not knowing how to be yourself can be difficult for some people. It's natural to want to be a part of society or be thought of in a positive way that leads to good outcomes. We don't want any negative energy around people, because it leads to problems.

The way I mimic someone is by acting how the other person would expect me to act, say what they would expect me to say, and do what they would expect me to do. By all means, be yourself, there is nothing wrong with that. The sad reality is, we climb the ranks in life to get noticed so that we can lead a better life. Being noticed is fortunate because its what customers are looking for; its what new potential partners seek; it's what the new boss relies on. Being yourself is great if you have a self-employed business, but ask yourself a question, how far would you get by being yourself at a Royal garden party? If you want to make things easier for yourself, then keep up to date with trends, do some homework, and go with the flow when necessary. Alternatively, let the chips fall where they may if you live a self-sustained life without answering to anyone. An example of mimicking, as I like to put it, is when someone bumps into me. I don't care who's fault it is, I apologise every time. It's not because I want to avoid a confrontation, it's because it defuses 99% of situations. Who cares if I'm conceded or not? Who cares if I look like a wimp? I have saved time, my life is stress-free, and I've deflected a problem by apologising for someone else's mistakes, putting their brain into a meltdown. Going with the flow, yet siding with the opposition can work wonders. People like to look for trouble; don't give them the satisfaction. If you can't beat them, join them.

"The smaller the detail, the greater the value."

– Doug Johnson

Tool 15. Being versatile

Being versatile and diverse in any situation, will no doubt be daunting when facing new challenges. It takes a lot of courage to trust your new intuition when you are already comfortable with the decisions you currently make in life. It's not just about solving problems; this is about you as a person. It's not easy going with new instincts based on what you already believe to be true, just, correct, or plausible. Before seeing a difference in your life, you need to address any hard-wired beliefs you might possess, by acknowledging that change is inevitable. Growth is optional, yet progress is impossible without change. Don't be that old man or woman cemented in their old ways because they know no different. Be as versatile as a slippery snake. Make positive changes to your personality to allow an understanding, become more accepting, and choose to live open-minded. There are ten essential values you need to adopt if you wish to get the results you want when facing problems:

1. Logic problem solving is not based on your personality, so don't include it.
2. Feelings, morals, or personal connections should never be considered, so don't get emotionally involved.

3. You need to accept facts and realities if you want to advance forward.
4. You need to stay disciplined and detached at all times.
5. You have to be ready to accept defeat or take losses for a greater advantage.
6. Believe and trust in the decisions you make, then follow them through logically.
7. Be prepared for disturbances, sudden changes, and new problem occurrences.
8. Have the positive mindset of a leader, a winner, and a champion.
9. Always have perseverance until you get to the end, the bottom, or to the root cause until no more problems occur.
10. Always act responsibly solving problems. Don't use your abilities to do harm, don't take advantage of others, and don't carry out evil acts.

Not only is this mindset challenging, it can be fun, creative, and there's never a dull moment. You can sit and wait for time to change an outcome in a situation, or you can play with all the possibilities until you find the best approach. That being said, it can be difficult staying neutral during a personal matter when you need to do the right thing. As I mentioned earlier, going with your head or heart will pull you in every direction possible. Nobody is telling you to act on your findings. It just means that you have arrived at a conclusion. Having the power, the resolve, and the know-how can be satisfactory enough without having to act at all. It's a wonderful feeling knowing that the power you possess can overcome many challenges. No one will have a clue about your new abilities, presuming you apply them. Here are a few more tips:

Tip 1

When the shit hits the fan, stay focussed, observant, and determined. Keep going. If you stop or give up halfway through the process, you will never get to the cause, and you will never solve the problem. If you need to back off for a while, that's fine. Generally, the problem will sit there until it's fixed.

Tip 2

Ignore people that might judge you, put you down, or make fun. This occurs when you act logically towards your goal. Where people like you and me see the big picture with a plan, others may see something that seems odd or indifferent.

Tip 3

Don't quit when more problems arise, yet know your capabilities. Because you are trying to get to the root cause, you will reveal new problems. Carry on solving them until there are no more problems. Just be careful who's toes you go stepping on, you don't want to reveal something that could cause you harm. Some roads are not worth going down in life.

Tip 4

If you need something or want something in life, resources will already exist to help you get it, you need to look by doing research.

Tip 5

If you can't come up with a plan and run out of ideas, it will come to you when you least expect it. The possibilities are endless, so you should be able to get creative in more ways than one. If you ever struggle, take a step back and look at the situation from another angle. There will always be a driving force or a connection, so at no point should you struggle for long.

Tool 16. Encouraging a change

This tool will remind you of pre-emptive action, but instead of taking action beforehand, we carry out specific activities that cause a situation to change during a problem, event, or encounter. Sound cool? Well, that's exactly what this is. It can be extremely beneficial. Here's why:

1. We can reveal information that we didn't know before, which serves our interest.
2. We can create a chain of events in our favour as an advantage.
3. We can overcome difficult problems that can't advance until there is a change or something new happens.
4. We can deflect problems away that might lead to a negative impact on our reputation, image, livelihood, or anything else we wish to protect.
5. We can change the direction the problem is going in.

A problem can be like a ring stuck on a finger. This tool represents the washing up liquid to lubricate the finger so that the ring will come off. When you are stuck in a jam, don't get disheartened by giving up. There are plenty of ways to cook an egg, you just need to get creative. Stop thinking like everyone else. Don't believe everything that you see. Sometimes the world is not how you perceive it, and people only show you what they want you to believe. We can take steps to break an image, presuming that's what it is, or we can change the path of the problem altogether. To do this, we need to use the reconnaissance tool to gather as much information as we can. We can use that information to find the characteristics, and the driving force behind the problem, so that we can play on what we know to be true. Without further ado, here's how specific actions can prompt a change in circumstances:

- Dragons' Den is a British television programme that allows entrepreneurs to present their business ideas to a panel of five wealthy investors. Once they have finished their pitch, they ask for a substantial amount of money in return for a stake in their company. If an entrepreneur makes a good pitch, one dragon or more will make an offer. Some savvy business ideas get presented anxiously before the negotiations tend to turn sour. The entrepreneurs either valuate their business wrong, offer a measly percentage to the dragons', or know nothing about the market they're in. The five Dragons' of 2019 are:

1. Deborah Meaden
2. Peter Jones
3. Touker Suleyman

4. Sara Davies
5. Tej Lalvani

Once a business has been presented, the dragons' need to decide if they are in or out. I cringe how some of the business models fail to cover basic aspects, or how the profit forecast reveals how narrow-minded the entrepreneur is. I don't want to burst anyone's bubble, but the lack of basic logic is often clear, which is a shame because they lose potential investors due to avoidable mistakes. To give you an example of how to encourage a change in a situation, our very own logic problem solver, Stacy, goes on the show to ask for forty thousand pounds in exchange for twenty percent of her business. If Stacy gets an offer from at least two dragons', she is going to encourage a change in the situation, so that one of the investors retracts their offer. Theoretically, Stacy doesn't need an investment because she has something more valuable than money, and that's her ability to solve problems. Even more so, If Stacy wanted all five dragons to invest, she would use her skills to achieve that confidently.

Stood tensely in front of the dragons' after finishing her pitch, along with any questions that needed answering, Stacy received an offer from Deborah and Touker. Knowing she only needed one dragon to invest, Stacy encouraged Deborah to retract her offer as a demonstration. From the knowledge she had about the show, knowing how Deborah had responded in the past, and using other useful details like expectation, Stacy decided to insulted Deborah's credibility. By saying she hasn't got much to offer live on camera, Deborah was outraged.

"Well, if you don't think that I have anything good to offer, then you won't be needing my money, so for that reason, I'm out. How dare you offend me!"

Stating such a comment was bound to get a negative response. Using what she knew, what was expected, and what would likely happen, she was able to convince Deborah with a high success rate to pull out. Stacy couldn't make spurious revelations about her business in case Touker and Deborah pulled out at the same time. Stacy successfully encouraged a change in the situation she was in. Now, let's view her situation from a logic problem-solving point of view. How can we describe the situation that an average person might not:

1. The problem, focus, or goal is to get one of the dragons to invest.
2. We are the ones that need, and the dragons are the ones that give.
3. It's one force against another with odds stacked against us.

4. There is a lot of pressure from having to stand up in front of five investors, while on television.
5. The five dragons' will know a lot about business, they have nothing to lose, and they are looking for a sustainable business to invest in.
6. The dragons' are humans, so they have emotions, and they respond differently.
7. The dragons' want to be impressed if they are going to hand over their money.
8. Each dragon will see one another as rivalries.
9. Each dragon will specialise in different types of business.
10. All of the dragons have certain expectations from entrepreneurs.

Don't forget; we are looking for advantages, weaknesses, and discrepancies to exploit. We can use this data to make a plan. Because it's a TV programme, we can study behaviour, learn how the dragons' respond, know who the dragons' are, what they do in their personal lives, and much more. If you want to achieve something, overcome a problem, or reach a goal, then at least do it properly. As you can see, there are plenty of smart ways to prompt a change in circumstances during a situation, you just need to get creative. Imagine this tool together with pre-emptive action? What a powerful combination that would be. These tools can be invaluable if used correctly, so practice and study as many times as you need to before it becomes second nature.

"You can't change what's going on around you until you start changing what's going on within you." - Zig Ziglar

Tool 17. Making connections

I genuinely believe that everything is connected in one way or another. Even if I'm wrong, ninety percent of the time I find something directly related. Keep in mind that we are talking about solving problems, pursuing goals, and carrying out ambitions. I frequently mention throughout this book about finding connections, but let me shed some more light on the subject, to make sure you don't take any shortcuts, or avoid missing out on any crucial findings. I use different references when I talk about connections, but let's look at some aspects of our lives:

- Families with brothers, sisters, and cousins etc, all share a connection through (blood)
- Millions of kids love slime sharing a connection through a (trend)
- Armies are created and come together to serve as a (duty)
- Search engine optimisation on the internet is a result of an (algorithm)
- Groups come together if they have the same (interest)

Depending on how strong these connections are, people, for example, might carry out actions motivated by expectation, necessity, or emotions leaving behind a kind of trail that is considered to you and me as a network of connections. We can then uncover and use them to our advantage. Revealing a network can help us work out people and situations. Try finding a link the next time you are faced with a challenge, task, or a problem. If you find anything slightly related, you will reveal how they are linked together. Even if you only find one connection, there could be a whole network that hasn't been discovered yet. Look how this problem below has a ton of connections starting with the conclusion as we work our way backwards:

Allan is in prison…

Because the judge sentenced him to serve three weeks…

Because the police arrested him for shoplifting…

Because he stole some food from a supermarket…

Because his family was hungry…

Because he lost his job…

Don't expect connections to correlate with time, and in sequence; they can happen at different times, for various reasons, and in different circumstances. We sometimes don't know the full story or understand why things happen in life, so we tend to act irrationally without knowing the whole story. By not seeing or knowing the entire picture, we can become arrogant and narrow-minded, reacting to a small piece of information. Arguments follow, fights break out, and bad decisions are made. Time, events, actions, decisions, needs and trends are all culprits, but they also allow us to find those related connections, which is excellent. Logic problem solvers don't need much to work with to achieve great results. The best thing about this tool is when your brain automatically makes those connections.

"All knowledge is connected to all other knowledge. The fun is making the connections." – Arthur Aufderheide

Seeing the whole picture

Once we have spent time studying the focus, problem, or cause using all of the skills you now possess, we can begin to build a picture. If you throw a pebble into a pond, the impact will create a ripple effect. Ripples are a direct consequence to the pebble hitting the water with force. It's the same when a stone shatters a window, or if someone stands on ice causing it to crack. In our case, the pebble represents the problem, and the ripples represent the connection, the characteristics, and any external factors. We have the ability to solve problems, and if we zoomed out, we would be able to see how many there are, which direction they are going in, and where they have come from. Once you see the big picture, you should have discovered a complete network and the goings-on, kind of like an ant farm or a network of roads that connect cities to towns. Within that information, you will discover weaknesses, discrepancies, and flaws that can lead you to solve the problem, presuming you act on it. With plenty of possibilities, you will have a better understanding, make better decisions, and in some cases, be happy and content with the information you have revealed. You can arrive at a satisfactory conclusion without needing to face the problem.

"Knowing is not enough; we must apply. Willing is not enough; we must do." - Johann Wolfgang von Goethe

Summary

Congratulations! You now have all the tools you will ever need to solve problems. I could create more that are complex, but for now, let's keep it simple. You are set to face any challenges that come your way, and you should fully understand the benefits of the tools, how to use them, and how to build a better life for yourself. This is not the end, but the beginning. Thank you for taking the time to read my book, and hopefully, you understand each tool enough to be able to apply them. The decisions you make in life are your responsibility, so this is as far as I can go. I can't solve your problems for you with this book alone, but the good news is, over 2020 I'm working on a website that will offer a course, Youtube videos on real-life events, a life coaching service, a blog, a Facebook group, and a store selling apparel. This book was published in November 2019, so please check to see if my website **logicproblemsolving.com** is live by the end of January. I'm so confident with this method, I plan on helping people become successful in every part of their lives from relationships, happiness, business and much more. Until then, I wish you the best of luck on your new journey.

Yours faithfully,

Joseph Kane

"To understand a problem, we need to dissect it, leave our comfort zone, then go on a necessary journey that we might not like" – Joseph Kane